Wildflowers

Wildflowers

a memoir of an inner city
high school teacher

Judy Fitch

authorHOUSE®

AuthorHouse™ *LLC*
1663 Liberty Drive
Bloomington, IN 47403
www.authorhouse.com
Phone: 1-800-839-8640

Karel Weir Lojowsky photographed Phillip Overton for the cover of Wildflowers.

A.C. Cerbelli is responsible for the graphics on the cover of Wildflowers.

Published by AuthorHouse   09/25/2013

ISBN: 978-1-4918-1375-1 (sc)
ISBN: 978-1-4918-1373-7 (hc)
ISBN: 978-1-4918-1374-4 (e)

Library of Congress Control Number: 2013916228

This book is dedicated to the memory of Emanuel Lawrence, one of the wisest old souls God ever created. He was a quiet observer, a preacher, and he always kept it real as he lived for his family. He had more love in him than anyone can imagine. He was a huge presence in a room and he captured my attention the first day I met him. People respected Emanuel even if they didn't know him; his opinions were welcomed and accepted. He leaves no children in his wake, for he never wanted to bring a child into this crazy world, however, I believe a child would have been very lucky to have had Emanuel Lawrence for a father. Rest in peace my sweet young man. You were appreciated and are missed every single day by everyone who knew you.

Sunrise 1989

Sunset 2013

Chapter 1

Introduction

We call it "The Valley". Those of us who are from here, know that once upon a time, millions of years ago, a glacier cut through the area, carving out our huge metropolitan park known as "The Valley". Games are played down there, roller blading is done down there, lots of 'making out' and drinking of beer is done down there. People sled, hike, kayak, cheat and meet down in the valley.

It's a beautiful place. One can come across deer, foxes, skunks, snakes, frogs, and lots and lots of flowers. Wildflowers. No one tends to them. No one fertilizes them. No one manicures their beds. They just grow. They are strong, beautiful, healthy, perennial wildflowers.

I am an English teacher, so I think in analogies, comparisons, and metaphors. I live in a wonderful little city, streets lined with houses, each with its own little yard. We are in the Midwest, so we have very distinct seasons. When the winter finally breaks, and spring has sprung, that is when we become reacquainted with our neighbors. Everyone seems to have the same mindset; get their yards in order. People are mowing, trimming, mulching, fertilizing, and generally manicuring their little slices of paradise. We run to the nurseries, purchase starter flowers and herbs, and begin to design what we've dreamed about all winter long. We weed and seed, and prune and fuss, using our specialty tools. We hire professionals and plan ahead as to the color schemes we intend to display in an unspoken contest with each other to win this year's "best yard". One can easily pinpoint those who have cheated and used Miracle Grow, the steroid for gardeners. This is what we do to produce our flowers, but unfortunately none of them are the best.

Why is it that the wildflowers growing in the valley always win the contest? No one's flowers are prettier, larger, stronger, or more

1

plentiful than those wildflowers, growing in the valley. Just imagine how these flowers would flourish if they were to be given the least bit of attention!

As a former high school English teacher in an inner-city setting, in the Midwest, this is how I've grown to view my students . . . . as wildflowers.

I've since retired and can sit back to reflect on my life as a teacher, on stage, influencing lives every day. I loved my job and they knew it. Every year, they knew it.

My one and only child, a son, went through my journey with me. He recalls that every fall, at the start of yet another school year, he would hear me lament, "These kids are different. I hate them. I'm never going to make it!"

Every fall his reply was the same, "Give it time, Mom. You know you always end up loving them." The boy was right. I always did. Each year beat the last. As the years went by, I became better and better at it. It was a gift. You had to love it. They had to love you. This was the secret, because if they loved you, there is nothing they wouldn't do for you, including trying Shakespeare!

People ask me what I miss now that I've retired. I miss the hugs, the group hugs, the individual hugs, the hugs from those kids who "came out" for the first time to me, the hugs from the girls who went into labor in my classroom, the hugs from the parents who heard from me, for the first time, how wonderful their child is.

I miss the attention I received every day. My classroom was my stage and I was the star. The hallways were my red carpet events. I was popular. I was afraid of no one. They loved me because I loved them. I was always smiling because I was so happy and secure in my world. Security guards often asked me why I was always smiling. They saw, more than most, teachers falling apart, being bullied, hating their jobs. I would tell them, "When I'm smiling, no one really knows what I'm thinking!"

Every now and then, security would come to my room responding to the noise. They'd laugh when they'd discover we were laughing or playing a game. We had so much fun.

Security would also come to my room in search of a fugitive. I would say I hadn't seen him or her, but all concerned knew darn well he or she was hiding under my desk! My room was a safe, soft place to fall.

I wasn't always so cocky and sure of myself. There were many events that if they had occurred later on in my journey, I'd have acted or reacted differently. I perfected my talents as events and years rolled by. No two days were ever alike. No two students were ever alike. Those students who were talked about in the teachers' lounges as "bad seeds" became my special projects, my personal challenges. Almost always the "bad seed" and I would end the year as the best of friends. It was a gift. After all, who could resist extra attention?

In my opening fall monologue, I always told my classes that they didn't know it yet, but they would end up loving me. One young man refused to give me a parting hug as they all did after class. Most just followed suit. Emanuel said, "I don't hug".

I said, "You will one day". He did. He is an adult now, still in touch, and has asked me to marry him!

My opening monologue also included the introduction of my one and only classroom rule: BE NICE OR GET OUT. It was self explanatory and really paid off. They would reprimand each other and school subsequent new arrivals if they weren't "Being nice". As I became more and more well known to the incoming students, they expected comedy. They made light-hearted fun of me trying to be a tough little white woman. When I was well enough established, and in front of juniors and seniors, I would tell them that if they were nice to me, there was nothing I wouldn't do for them, including change a grade. Come to me and we will talk, however, if you fuck with me, I will go downstairs to the office and make things up about you. Who do you think they will believe, you or me? Got it? They always were horrified and laughed like crazy, but they really didn't know how serious I was.

I was serious about the changing of a grade. I told my classes that if they were ever in danger, due to a grade from me, there is always something that can be done. The importance of a letter grade on a report card was no match for some unreasonable physical act administered by an unruly parent. Deals can be made. Changes can be made. Extra credit can be given. I wanted no one hurt over a letter on a piece of paper given by me. In my thirty year career I can remember only one sad student coming to me with such a request.

Either only one was in danger or only one wanted even me to know of a crazy parent committing acts of child abuse.

I informed the students that they never had to do anything they didn't want to do in my class. I never knew who had had a bad morning. I never knew who didn't feel well or was hungry. I never wanted to embarrass or humiliate anyone. For instance, no one ever wants to be put on "front street" to reveal their less than perfect reading skills. No one wants to be forced to speak when they don't have the answer. No one wants to be forced to read his or her paper aloud if he or she doesn't want to. It's a matter of simply being respectful to each student and his rights. Reading aloud is one event that can cause immense anxiety. For those who cannot read like a machine gun, it can cause embarrassment and stuttering. Everyone always had the right of refusal in my classes. In doing so, I found that many would volunteer, which would in turn, prod others on. I taught them that there is a secret to reading aloud. The secret to reading aloud is to read painfully slowly, thus aiding in the audience's understanding. I demonstrated as if I were reading to a group of pre-schoolers, with lots of inflection and enthusiasm. Then I would read like a machine gun and ask which one they better understood and preferred. By reading slowly, one can hit every word, take breaths, look up at the audience and have everyone receive the message.

It takes a certain personality to connect with teenagers. Don't get me wrong, one must know his or her stuff, so to speak, because teenagers are wise little folks and can see through a fraud. I realize that not everyone who becomes a teacher can have the delivery of a stand-up comedian, or the looks of a beauty queen. I'm just saying, it doesn't hurt. If you are easy on the eye, and can make it fun, who wouldn't want to be in your presence? Somewhere along the line I acquired this wonderful quote, "People like people, who make them feel good, about themselves." This is so wonderfully true and useful, especially with teenagers.

Being easy on the eye can simply mean a smiling face, clean clothes, and all your teeth! I was told more than once by my African-American wildflowers, that they were under the impression most white people smell like wet dogs or bologna sandwiches. Upon hugging me, this myth was dispelled.

Kids are funny! When something is funny, I laugh. When I would inquire as to whether they make their mom's laugh, the answer was usually, "No, I don't be funny in front of her." Laughing has such a cleansing effect on one's soul. The kids knew they could get to me with their humor. They knew I could be distracted with their humor. Laughter is infectious and good for the morale of a class.

A valuable lesson I learned from a young, black, male principal was that these kids are very much accustomed and immuned to screaming and yelling. For many wildflowers, it is the norm. In the classroom, screaming and yelling was never the way one was going to reach them. It was those of us whose deliveries were whispered or soft-spoken that would see results. Loud begets louder begets loudest and then it's on! The teacher cannot lose. The student cannot lose. The class loves it. It's just like home. Security is summoned and someone must leave. The rest of the class period is a wash. It could have been handled with finesse and quiet dignity, ending with laughter. A good response to a loud kid would be, "I can feel your pain and frustration. Talk to me. Let it out. I understand." Who could hate that? It works. Everyone needs to be heard, especially frustrated teenagers. If one is not used to being heard, when someone listens, it stops whomever in his tracks. It is so foreign that it gets the attention and the respect of the whole class. I also took every opportunity to admit when I'd made a mistake. I loved for a student to correct me. It makes the teacher more human, real, and lovable. This was not part of the curriculum taught in college, it was part of the school of hard knocks. Each year one becomes better and better.

Chapter 2

Background

I graduated in 1971 from Bowling Green State University, in Bowling Green, Ohio. I was an aspiring math major. I had always loved algebra. Finding the missing piece to the puzzle was always so rewarding. In order to return as an algebra teacher, one had to jump through an enormous number of hoops, hoops my brain could not handle. Back in the 60's, math classes were heavily populated with men. I often found myself the only girl in the class. I also found my brain stuck and unable to function at these necessary upper levels. After sweating a lot, and cheating to survive, I changed my major to English. After all, I could read.

What a blessing changing my major to English was to me in the long run. With reading and writing, I could always manage to engage my classes in conversations about what they would have done differently than whomever we were reading about at the time. I told them that writing is just a way of talking with a pencil. They all have opinions; they all have biases. They all could identify at some point, and on some level, with some character.

If there had been a suggestion box at my university, I had a few suggestions. In those days, student teaching was required, but at the very end of one's four year stint. Big mistake! Huge!

I was placed in an all white, middle class, middle school, or junior high, as it was called back in the dark ages, with two other female teacher hopefuls. I flourished and was ultimately offered a position, however, the other two soon learned of their stage fright! They both had huge problems being in front of a crowd . . . . even a crowd of twelve year olds. Neither finished. Both discovered, a bit too late, that teaching was not for them. Student teachers should be shown the ropes much more early on, so as to have a chance to re-route their talents and not waste too much time and money doing so.

Chapter 3

First teaching assignment

I spent two years at this junior high, flailing around like the rookie that I was. I was more interested, as a twenty-two and twenty-three year old, in my personal life, maybe a male teacher or two, and certainly where I was headed for my spring break!

This assignment is where I learned that there are desperate, needy wildflowers everywhere looking for a hero. An eighth grader named Sondra was a little on the odd and shy side. She wore her coat every day, all day. Sondra revealed to me in a poem that she was pregnant. The father of her unborn child was her older brother. Sondra was a motherless child left in the care of her father, a man who worked long hours in order to provide for his children. She was, on occasion, discussed in our teachers' lounge, because the year before I arrived, she had attempted suicide. I recall a cynical, female physical education teacher saying that she'd done it for attention. My simplistic addition to this conversation was that somebody should have given it to her. This is where I learned that the old-timers often regard rookies as bleeding hearts that think they can change the world, and save all the kids. Change the world? No. Save somebody? Maybe. Make fun of a desperate teenager's suicide attempt? Never. I remember going to those in charge and turning it over. Sondra's brother went to prison for rape and incest and she had the baby.

This school is also where I learned to be very careful when it came to calling a student's home. There was a seventh grade boy who came to school every day with a brief case in tow. The puzzling thing was that he never had what he needed for class. I asked Russell to open his brief case for me one day, only to find it was full of candy! I thought that and he was adorable and couldn't wait to share this with his parents, whom we were always encouraged to contact. Russell came to school the next day with a broken arm.

You've heard of "letting sleeping dogs lie"? I learned to let sleeping kids lie. A rather large young boy had fallen asleep while I was busy teaching. When I shook him in an attempt to awaken him, he woke with a violent thrashing that landed on my jaw. I was later informed of the meds he was taking, and was advised to let him sleep.

My second year out of the gate is when I experienced the loss of a student, three to be exact. It was Halloween. There was a junior high school party. An older boy, whom we later learned had developmental issues, showed up with a car. Four of my wild little female students decided to go for a ride. One headed back to the party because she'd forgotten her purse. They left without her. Lucky for her, because the other three girls and the driver all died in the valley when the car hit a tree at a very high rate of speed. This took place on a Friday. On Monday morning, the principal entered my room before the students arrived to give me the sad news of the seats that would that day, and forever more, be empty. One by one, the mothers came to retrieve the contents of their daughters' lockers. I remember feeling numb.

Having been married my senior year of college, I was a young bride the first year in that building. I was a young divorcee the second year. Four of the young, single teachers and I headed to Fort Lauderdale for spring break. It was after that vacation, that I decided to quit my first teaching position, withdraw my meager retirement funds, and head for the tropics. Living in Florida had been a long time dream of mine. Always tan. Always warm. Always able to go to the beach. For a girl from the Midwest, this was wonderful. I lived in a hotel above a corner ice cream store. It cost $35 a week and that included maid service!

Chapter 4

A move to Florida

A teacher works the school year, but receives checks throughout the summer. That, plus my retirement money (which I would come to regret withdrawing) enabled me to become a beach bum. I was loving life. I swam alone at night. This was prior to the movie, "Jaws", which educated everyone as to how fool-hearty it was to do so. I wore gold jewelry into the water. I splashed and played, because I didn't have a care in the world. The sharks must have been busy elsewhere, because my behavior was absolutely calling them! God was watching over me for sure.

Because I was so enjoying my beach bum lifestyle, I had no interest in securing a full time teaching position which I was offered while substituting in Fort Lauderdale. I'll never forget a middle school in the Everglades. I was hired to substitute as a home economics teacher. The students were predominantly African-American which was new to me at the time. I remember circulating the room, leaning in and over to chat and assist wherever I was needed. There was a little girl who wore her hair in corn rows. The parts of her hair were like busy highways with what seemed like thousands of bugs running through them. I was horrified. I couldn't wait to get to the school nurse to get some help for this child. The school nurse calmly looked at me and asked, "What do you want me to do about it?"

"Clean her up! Fix this mess! Help her! Do something!" I must have come across as a nut to her. She simply and calmly replied, "Now, we could clean her up, but she will go home to the same house, with the same family, the same furniture, and the same bed, and she will return with the same problem tomorrow." I was traumatized and never returned.

I did, however, accept positions at other schools. At another junior high is where I met a chubby, little sixth grade boy by the name of Waddel. There was a bomb scare called in to this particular school, long before bomb scares became fashionable. The entire student body emptied into the playground. We were out in that steamy playground for hours. I didn't quite understand why they just didn't send us all home, until it was explained to me that if they were to dismiss everyone, that will only ensure another bomb scare would be called in tomorrow! While out in that damned playground, I was chatting with Waddel. He said, "If I was planning to bomb a school, I would call it in, wait for everyone to empty into the playground . . . . and then I would blow up the playground!" I thought Waddel was a genius. A little scary, but a genius!

G-Mann

The high school in southern Florida where this story took place was in an infamous area, known for its serious drug problems. The only white faces were members of the faculty, of which there were just a few. Our powerful black, male principal was ever-present and involved with his wildflowers. The annual talent show, presented for the parents and general public, is where this wonderful principal performed his marvelous rendition of "I Found My Thrill on Blueberry Hill".

G-Mann was a thug. I did not have him in a class. Everybody knew G-Man. I was under the impression that the "G" stood for "gang". He had money and a girlfriend. His name and bullets shot from a gun were professionally etched around his head. He was a nice, polite, young thug. Teachers liked him and students respected him. He was a senior. He was "The man".

One morning, while the buses were unloading, G-Mann's girlfriend appeared out of nowhere and shot him in his head. He went down like a bag of bricks. It was horrifying and surreal. Rumor was that he had cheated on her. Shocker!

 ## Substitute Teaching

Substitute teaching has its perks. One can refuse jobs, request certain schools or grade levels, remain free to pursue other avenues. My lifelong best friend, Sue, finally joined me in Florida and together we pursued waitressing and modeling. You only live once. Right? Opportunities were abundant in southern Florida for girls like us. We did some runway work. I was in the background of a movie that was filmed on a cruise ship, and was in the courtroom scene of a movie called "Lenny" starring Dustin Hoffman. It was filmed in the Fort Lauderdale courthouse and we lunched in the parking lot of the courthouse where we milled around with the star. I was very impressed with him as well as with myself. Life was good.

Returning home once in a while, like for Christmas, was fun. Seeing my family and friends, but mostly having them see me, was a treat. One such visit resulted in my meeting the man who would eventually become the father of my wonderful son. When Sue and I were returning to Florida after our Christmas visit, I asked him to make arrangements to join us. Big mistake! Huge! Because he did. We both felt trapped. Looking back, we realize we were the worst possible people for each other, but our son was the result of that toxic relationship so we both agree we would do it all over again.

Our roommate, Sue, left to find herself out West and our toxicity escalated. He left for home up North and I eventually followed, in search of ways to fix everything. Yes, we married, but we lived apart, due to fights, more than we lived together. During a lengthy separation, his mother died a very painful death due to bone cancer. He called me to be by his side for the funeral. That was the night we conceived our son.

Chapter 5

Return to the Midwest

I had my trusty teaching license, and began substitute teaching during my pregnancy. It was pretty bad. Unhappiness at home permeates every aspect of one's life. I never knew, until the call came in, what school I'd be sent to or what I'd be teaching. When our baby was born, however, my husband was working as a paramedic. Life was never good, or happy, or relaxed. When our son was eighteen months old, we divorced. On the same day my lawyer called to tell me that the divorce was final, I was hired for a half day teaching position, provided I'd also assume the thankless job as cheerleader coach. My next call was to a girlfriend who agreed to be my half day babysitter. This all happened in one day. This assignment was in an all white, upper middle class suburb populated by lots and lots of yuppies and kids with fast cars. I celebrated sixteenth birthdays with a boy whose folks bought him a boat, and another who was gifted an addition onto his bedroom. Here is where I learned that many professionals look down their noses at the teaching profession, and, as a result, so do their children. It was a rough year. I had a baby at home and a job that intimidated me. I simply felt I didn't fit in. The athletic director was a young, single man who showed interest in me. We went out maybe twice, but in the end, he married one of the graduating senior girls.

As the cheerleader coach, I had many duties and spent lots of hours with these girls. One girl in particular, posed a constant problem, so during spring tryouts for the next year, I saw to it that she did not make it. She did not qualify. The girl was either late or absent from games and practices alike. She arrived drunk to a game. She was a nightmare. Due to a declining enrollment, my half day gig had been eliminated. I'd already received my lay-off papers so my motivation was to eliminate this problem for the incoming coach, whomever that may have been. The following day, due to this cheerleader's demise, I was summoned to the principal's office. I was greeted by the principal, the girl's father, and the father's lawyer! I was horrified and appalled by this outrageous over-reaction to my decision and I told them so. What were they going to do, fire me? She was reinstated as cheerleader for the following year, however, I was later informed that she couldn't fulfill her duties as cheerleader due to the fact that she had become pregnant! Sorry Daddy.

Chapter 6

First Inner City Assignment

I found myself, once again in the substitute circus. I was earning anywhere from $18 to $22 per day, and these were not easy days. Someone informed me that I could earn twice as much if I were to sub in the inner city. My first reaction was that this was out of the question, but I got my wheels turning, put one foot in front of the other, and before I knew it, I was called to my very first inner city school. There were many Hispanic students, and white kids, the likes of which I'd never experienced before. I loved it and soon I was hired as a "building sub". This meant a full time position in one school, where I covered for whomever was absent that day. As a result, I came to know most of the kids, most of the teachers, and I had what is known as "a foot in the door".

Mrs. Baker was an English teacher for whom I was covering due to her extended absence. Sadly, she died and I was now a full time inner city high school teacher. I was part of the big machine. This was the year that busing was mandated, so as to ensure an equal education for all students. One day I had all white and Hispanic students. The next day I had all black students. I don't know who was more scared, them or me.

For as long as busing lasted, it was a farce. Children need to be near home. The sad stories related to and about busing are many. Many of the parents did not own cars, consequently being summoned to retrieve an ill child, or to attend a game after school, or to participate in school conferences, was simply out of the question.

Schools sponsored incentive contests during parent-teacher conferences. A token prize and school-wide recognition was given to that special teacher who had hosted the most parents.

I must say, I usually won these contests. I took it seriously and it had been proven to me that meeting the parents or care-givers usually provided a wealth of information about that student. The weekend prior to a parent-teacher conference event, I would devote to calling everyone on my class lists, sometimes over 165 students, to extend a personal and heartfelt invitation to our conference evening. Phones are considered a luxury and during a lean month, those particular bills are overlooked. As a result, phone numbers are constantly changing. The number of parents I actually was able to extend a personal invitation to was probably half of the list. All who had been reached, however, accepted the invitation with effusive thank yous and their word that they wouldn't miss it for the world.

The big night arrived. After all was said and done, and all the lists were tallied, like I said, many times I would be the winner, the most celebrated teacher! I won that night for hosting five parents, yes, just five parents had attended this conference regarding their wonderful kids.

The Day Care Center

There was a day care center in the school for those students who had babies. On one occasion, a ninth grader who arrived with her six week old baby girl, dropped her off and went on about her ninth grade day. I carpooled with the head of this day care center, so I spent lots of after school time there. On this particular afternoon, the young mother had gone with the flow and jumped on her bus and was off . . . . without her daughter! Now, here was the problem. It was a forty-five minute ride to her home. Her mother had no car and no idea where the school was even located. We were forced to call the authorities to come for this child. We waited for several hours before someone arrived.

On yet another occasion, a young mom dropped her child off for the school day. She then left the building to go spend the day downtown to do some last minute Christmas shoplifting. She, too, never returned. The grandmothers were no help, with no car, and no idea where the school was located, once again, we were forced to call the authorities.

Evelyn

At first glance, in our day care center, one would hope that these mothers would, at least be seniors. This was not the case. The vast majority of our young mothers were our ninth graders, who became pregnant while in middle school. On two separate occasions, ninth grade girls went into labor in my classroom. Evelyn's water broke. The child was scared speechless. She was a beautiful young girl who was kicked out of her lesbian mother's house due to this pregnancy. She was "staying" with her baby's daddy's family. Evelyn was a very mature and popular girl who did not enjoy her pregnancy. She complained to me about her aches and pains. If she needed to use the restroom, she didn't even need to ask. If she needed to roam around the classroom because her back hurt, she could. She was constantly hungry and we all brought treats for Evelyn. The entire class went through this pregnancy with her . . . . right up until the day her water broke right in the middle of "Romeo and Juliet"! She asked me not to leave her side. The paramedics arrived to a little girl in full blown labor. At this point, the female principal was on board and accompanied her to the hospital. She had a healthy baby girl that she named Porsha. Not long after she delivered this baby and was living with the baby's daddy's family, did he bring a gun to a basketball game, was arrested, and began serving his sentence.

Porsha is around ten now and looks just like her beautiful mother. As far as I am aware, she has moved on from her jailbird boyfriend. She always joked that she wanted to marry a white guy, "Cuz that be where the money is".

Yvette

A couple of years after Evelyn's labor and delivery was Yvette's sad story. She was a cute little girl enrolled in our special education program and was mainstreamed into my class. She had a learning disability but she had no disabilities when it came to boys. She was extremely well developed and dressed the part. I kept my eye on her because I worried. I had a talk with her about birth control when I became aware she had a special boyfriend. I even had a heart to heart with him . . . all to no avail because she eventually became pregnant. She, however, was a junior. She strutted the halls with all the pride of an expectant mother. She was completely absorbed in her boyfriend and he in her. We watched her five foot frame gain way too much weight eating all the wrong junk foods. She'd lost all interest in school, only attended to see her friends and her boyfriend, passing the time until it happened. It was her eighth month and she had cut a class to remain with me because she didn't feel well. She was sleeping on her desk when she awoke crying. Yes, her water broke, and she became hysterical. Once again, the paramedics were summoned and took her away on a stretcher, crying. Her sister happened to be in this class and accompanied her to the hospital. Her boyfriend was alerted and followed on his own. She gave birth to a tiny baby girl, who only lived for five days.

A month later, when Yvette returned to school, she brought with her a picture of this infant in her tiny casket to show all her teachers and friends. It was pitiful. She did not seem to have the emotions that went along with this excruciating scenario. She was removed and aloof. It was strange and seemed like she enjoyed the attention she received from her sad story. Yvette remained obese and eventually, of course, the boyfriend faded away.

So very many of the new moms in these schools wanted to show off their newborns and would sneak them in the school and up to their classrooms. More than a few times my class was interrupted by the entrance of a mom with her six week old infant. This is what I mean about the mothering given by a teenager. These busy, dangerous, and dirty hallways were no place for a six week old baby, but the need to show them off was a powerful motivator. I have many, many pictures of me teaching a class, holding a newborn in my arms like it was normal! I always escorted the moms out afterward and pleaded with them to be careful. There is almost nothing one can teach these young moms who already think they know it all.

Busing

When I thought of busing, I thought of how it directly affected my high schoolers. The fact of the matter was that the elementary students were being bused too. The ones picked up first, sometimes spent more than an hour on that bus before arriving at school. Many had wet their pants. Many became car sick and threw up during the ride. It was miserable for the kids, the drivers, and the teachers who had to pick up the pieces of these sad, scared, and embarrassed little children.

Busing did not cut down on the class cutting either. Having no knowledge of the new neighborhoods in which they found themselves, simply meant that they didn't go far. They chose to invade neighbors' garages to gather and somewhat terrorize these residents.

After many years of trying to put this square peg into the round hole, busing was disbanded. The students could now attend their neighborhood schools or choose a magnet school for which they were given bus tickets. Now, the athletes were playing on teams with their friends, parents at least knew where the school was, and a sort of comfort zone was re-established.

As far as sports, I never understood, at first, why these schools rarely had winning teams. Outsiders would think, as I did, that with all these big, strong, ruthless young boys, they should be able to kick ass against any team they played. This was not the case. It soon was revealed to me the reasons why. These are boys and girls who never had anyone with whom to throw the ball around in their yards. They never played catch with Dad. They probably were not used to playing games of any kind. They had no sense of team spirit or good sportsmanship. During busing, as well as after, the spectators were predominately the faculty members whom the kids begged to come and watch them play. Their parents, once again, couldn't get to the games. I watched fights break out, not only on the field, but on the benches, between our own teammates! The other teams watched in amazement. Our teams had little or no self control. They were not only learning the basic skills, but they were learning how to be a team. Then there was the matter of attendance at their practices and the morale factor of a losing team. They had to withstand the constant harassment from the student body, due to their losing streaks. It was the faculty and their coaches who truly appreciated what it took for those boys who stuck with it.

 Tiffany

Tiffany was a white girl who truly impressed me. She would speak of how she was "grounding" herself for getting a little too wild. She was the daughter of a pill-popping mother where a definite role-reversal had taken place. Her mother moved away and she took up residence with her dad. One day after school, she returned to the building in a panic. When she had arrived home to her corner apartment, all of their less than wonderful belongings were on the curb. They had been evicted. What could I do? What would anyone do? I took her home with me. She lived with my son and me for a few months until she took off with her boyfriend who was joining the navy in North Carolina. She married and divorced that guy, but not until she'd had a son with him. Years later, I received a call from her new husband and a cousin, who were planning a surprise birthday party for Tiffany. I was to be the surprise! They flew me down and we had a wonderful reunion and surprise party. As the years have gone by, I have come to learn that Tiffany had developed a serious drinking problem and has all the issues that go along with it.

Home away from home

This particular school had a longstanding good reputation in our city, however, things change. It went from being run almost like a military school, to a breeding ground for criminals! We had everything from a horticulture department to the day care center I mentioned. There were tunnels and secret hallways. One day while I was heading toward the horticulture rooms and the greenhouse, I ran into a couple of thugs smoking some reefer. Not knowing exactly what to do or how to handle this situation, I simply said, "Give me that!" The guys looked at me, laughed, and said, "Why you trippin', Girl?" I left.

Before Mrs. Baker died and left me in charge, one of my assignments as the building sub was as the temporary horticulture teacher. I had to do quite a bit of preparation in order to fulfill this tall order. One never wanted to let the kids know one was lost. There were quite a few Asian students: Chinese, Cambodian, Filipinos, Vietnamese, and Korean. One young man sitting in front of me was totally lost every day. He had no command of the language and was breaking my heart. He was so pitiful that I offered my time to him after school to go over everything at his own pace. What a wonderful giving teacher I was. This went on for weeks. We spent hours together just working on his English skills. No one knew of this because we were tucked away in the horticulture department far away from everybody else. I needed to be praised for going the extra mile, so I brought it up in our teachers' lounge. To my great surprise, everyone started laughing hysterically at me. I was totally confused by their reaction until someone informed me that this young man was born and raised in the city and this was his "game" with new teachers! He had completely conned me into spending my time with him. He knew the language better than I! The thing that got to me the most was that the other students went along with this scam and let me be the fool. These are the things one goes through as a rookie. Teachers must certainly pay their dues.

Achieving seniority within this huge school system was not an easy thing to do. There were constant budget cuts and the teaching staff was always the first to go. Usually we received our pink slips toward the end of the school year, and then our contracts were simply not re-issued. Plans had to be made for unemployment, and odd jobs taken, in order to survive until one's name reached the top of the all mighty re-hire list.

My son was enrolled in a neighborhood karate class. Not only did I attend all events, but I was there for all classes and practices as the resident helicopter mom. The other side of this karate school offered tanning beds. During my, almost year long lay-off, I ran these tanning beds for minimum wage. My hours were long, but I loved the hands on responsibilities of the clients and being on board for my son.

After a year, I was rehired and sent to a middle school. Most teachers will agree that teaching at the middle school level is merely a way of paying one's dues. Many people don't even enjoy their own children at that difficult age. I was so very happy to have received this call that I showed up well dressed in my white business suit and heels. I was greeted and shown the ropes by the school librarian, whose first words to me were that I would soon need to come out of those shoes. Due to a shortage of classrooms, I was escorted to what had been a kitchen for their former home economics department, but would now serve as my English classroom. Wonderful! The students were seated at round tables which accommodated six each. Wonderful! Ovens with bottom loading broilers were within reach of almost everyone. Wonderful! More often than I would care to admit, a book was placed in a broiler and turned on. Wonderful! The smoke! The flames! The embarrassment! Wonderful!

On my first day, I witnessed the assistant principal being slammed to the ground as the buses were loading. In his attempt to break up a fight, his collar bone was broken and he was out of commission for six weeks. Also on that first day, as I was being escorted around by the librarian, above us, on the third floor, a fight broke out. Anyone could tell it was a fight by the banging, slamming, and yelling we could hear. Everyone loves a good fight. Lots of cheering and egging on. The reality of this fight was revealed when we were informed it was a fight between two female teachers! Believe it. The stress is sometimes insurmountable.

This assignment was where I became accustomed to carrying a stick, formerly known as a pointer. Of course, I never hit anyone, but the threat was always there, and slamming it next to someone was always so much fun. Turning one's back was never a good idea because this always presented an opportunity for a student to do something, anything, just to prove he or she could. One little boy whose name was Lamar was a particular pain in my neck. Although it was frowned upon to put anyone in the hall, because then he or she would become a problem for the halls, we all resorted to it out of a need to preserve our sanity. Lamar was kicked to the hall on one fine day. It was either that, or kill him, so out he went. Soon, someone noticed a note being pushed under the door. The note was, of course, for me and it read: MS. FITCH IS UGLY! I thought that was the cutest thing I'd seen in a very long time. I took

MRS
Fitch
is ungly

it home and framed it and hung it on my kitchen wall, serving as quite the conversation piece.

Later on, when I was teaching in the county's infamous juvenile detention center, that I affectionately refer to as the 'slammer', I ran across Lamar. The inmates were escorted into our classrooms with their hands behind their backs. They filed by the teachers' desks, depositing their I.D. cards as they headed to their seats. It was not until I saw the name did I recognize him, as it was a few years later and he was quite grown up. I asked if he remembered me and of course, he did. I asked if he remembered the note he'd slipped under the door for me and of course, he did. The next day I brought it in to show him I'd not only kept it, but I had framed it. He smiled and I shared it with the class. All day long, officers and teachers stopped in to see this sweet note. By the end of the day he had had enough flack from the guys and asked me to take it home.

I paid my dues at the middle school level in more than a few ways. From our school parking lot, my car was stolen. It was a big, blue Buick, a gift from my parents. Unless you've had a car stolen, you cannot know how surreal the feeling of seeing that the spot where you parked, is now empty. It was discovered after school, of course, when I wanted to go home. I circled around and around until I became aware of the reality of the situation. The police were called. A group of students approached when they saw how upset I was. These kids told the officers where to look for the car, and they found it. It needed some work, because of the handiwork done with a huge screw driver, that was left in my car. It was discovered that the perp was an older brother of one of those kids. He had targeted my car because of the leather purse sitting on the back seat. The purse was on its way to the leather repair shop directly after school that day. That purse was what made my car so much more attractive than others in that lot. Insurance took care of the damage, but the car never really felt the same again. This became yet another spontaneous cautionary tale about being aware of how opportunists perceive what's on one's back seat!

It was then that I began soliciting advice from my students as to the type of car they and their boyz were not interested in stealing. I was leasing and driving into the hood five days a week. I wanted to never repeat the feeling that day of not seeing my ride home where I'd left it. For years, adhering to their valuable advice, I drove an Impala. I was never bothered again. After retirement, my first purchase was a Mini Cooper, convertible, of course.

Jade

While teaching in middle school I met Jade. Jade was the youngest mom I'd ever had in class. She was a problem girl, but we got along famously. Teachers were always on the alert for any and all weapons the kids may have had. There was an occasion, during a locker sweep, that I found a meat clever in Jade's locker. When I asked what she had this for, she simply replied, "For protection".

When her baby girl was born, she invited me to visit her in the projects. I put on my brave hat and ventured deep into the projects one day after school. This entire visit was completely surreal. She met me in the parking lot with an uncle, whose job it was going to be to guard my car. As we climbed the nasty stairway, all I could smell was the strong odor of wine and urine. There were concrete block walls and wire fencing along the balconies. When we entered the apartment where she lived with her mother and two little brothers, her mother never once acknowledged me. The two little brothers never looked up from the television. These little boys were seven and eight years old and were watching hard core pornography. I could not believe my eyes. If this was the norm, it would explain any violence in the dating scene of these young people. Is this their introduction to love, relationships, dating, and marriage? It explained so much for me. I found it extremely sad for those boys who lost their innocence much too early. It can be said here that when one knows better one does better. If this particular incident had happened later in my career I know I would have done something about the living conditions of those children, however, then I simply walked away. Of this I am not proud.

A personal and regretful experience happened while I was teaching in the detention center. There was a sweet, young corrections officer, that, contrary to my own rules, I chose to meet for a date. He'd been so sweet, respectful, polite, humble, and persistent. He never called me anything but Ms. Fitch. He always complimented my special "ways" with the kids. I liked him and felt he was worth an evening. He'd invited me to his apartment for a dinner. I arrived and he showed me around his lovely apartment. The music was playing and I could smell the dinner cooking. Then, in his pathetic attempt at being romantic, he took me by the shoulders, threw me up against a livingroom wall, and tried to kiss me. It was like a scene from a bad movie. I used my toughest, most forceful voice to tell him he had one second to let me go and to open the door so I could leave, or he would be so sorry.

As I was driving home from this man-handling event, I was reminded of Jade's little brothers. Because this man let me go, stepped back with a look of confusion on his face, I don't think he thought he was doing anything wrong. Perhaps he was someone who got his information from pornography.

In school the following Monday, he was his normal, polite self, like nothing at all had happened. It dawned on me that perhaps he thought of me as a bit emotionally unstable. As I reflect on this unfortunate event, I know I could have handled it much differently, and perhaps have taught him a little something about the art of courting and love making from a totally different perspective. I wish I'd had my wits about me to use it as a teachable moment, however, the fear took over.

Never judge a book by its cover

Another time when I was laid-off, my name was spotted by the principal from a neighboring suburb as having seen it before. I guess he took pity on me and gave me a call for a position as a ninth and tenth grade English teacher. This was an all white community. The board of education, the middle school, and the high school were all housed in one building. Everyone was on a first name basis. I taught there for two years and had a wonderful experience, until their declining enrollment dictated yet another lay-off for me. While there, I enjoyed the staff, the students, and the location. The teachers' lounge is where I learned to knit. Many of the women were accomplished knitters and they taught me all their tricks of the trade. The queen of this knitting circle was a revered veteran teacher. We were quite a group.

This veteran teacher was married to a coach in this school system. They were an older, childless couple who were treated as royalty. While knitting, she would brag about her huge Sunday dinners, every Sunday, prepared for anyone and everyone who may stop by, mainly members of the football team. They created their own family, year after year, and loved doing it. They felt loved and needed and oh so well respected. She attended all the games, and her husband was in charge of it all. They owned a place in the South where she would spend her off time, usually on her own, because his duties were year round. They were both nearing retirement and looking forward to the next phase of their lives together.

Before they could retire in the lap of luxury afforded by two teachers' retirements, the unmentionable happened. Mr. Wonderful Coach was indicted for child sexual abuse of his past and present football team members. It was an awful scandal for this school and community. Their Sunday afternoon dinners involved more than his wife was aware. It was not until well after graduation and adulthood that these victims came forward, as is usual for this crime. It was thought that no one would have believed that this pillar of the school and community would have been committing such disgusting crimes against these boys. He was charged and sent to prison. His wife left for her home in the South. I do not know if she stood by her man or not. I do know, however, that her dreams of retirement were shattered.

Not a year later, in the same system, their drama director was charged and sent to prison for the very same crime. I was no longer a member of this faculty, so all I knew was what everyone else knew from reading the newspaper articles. It is all too true that one can never judge a book by its cover. This sweet, little middle class school system would never be the same after these events. We live in an age where we must be aware of our surroundings and probably trust no one, especially those whom we entrust with our most prized possessions . . . our children. It's difficult to explain that those who are the nicest to us, are the ones we need to be aware of the most. Some of these nice people certainly have a diabolical agenda directed at the most vulnerable in our society.

The 'fix up'

One of my students in this sweet school wanted to "fix me up" with his father, who was single, as was I. He brought me some pictures to prove what a handsome man his dad was. He was more than handsome. He was movie star good looking! The young man informed me that his father would be released from prison a year from that coming June and would really like to meet me! Wow!

This was when a cautionary tale was born, and a teachable lesson, not only for my son and his friends, but for my classes throughout the years. This boy's handsome father was involved in a run of the mill bar fight. The only thing that went wrong was that someone was killed when his head hit the curb. This student's dad was charged with murder and had been behind bars for most of his sons' lives. The follow up to this story was that after he was released, because he had a felony on his record, he could not secure employment. He soon became involved in drug trafficking, was caught, and returned to prison. The biggest losers in this family were his sons, and, of course the grandmother who raised them. I was introduced to this man while he was free because he attended a parent-teacher event at the school, however, a love connection was not made. Teachers have a responsibility to maintain their dignity and reputations at all costs. It would never have been a good idea, but my bar fight story that resulted, which many can identify with, including my own son and his friends, made him a valuable person in my career. Anyone can find himself involved in a bar fight. Anyone's head can hit a corner or a curb. Anyone can die from a head injury. When someone ends up dead, someone has to pay the price. This man's life, the lives of his entire family, and the family of the deceased, were forever changed after that unfortunate bar fight.

The 'Melting Pot'

Each time I was rehired,. I managed to make my way back to what I always called my home school. It was my first inner city assignment and therefore I achieved a level of comfort. I loved the diversity of the students and faculty and felt I truly fit in.

This wonderful school was known as "The Melting Pot". Every nationality under the sun was represented. Every May first we held a celebration known as "Nationality Day". The television stations and newspapers covered this massive event. The day began with an alphabetical parade beginning with our American Indian population. Dressed in their cultural garb and demonstrating their dance, it was an awesome start to an awesome day. Following this lengthy parade, everyone was dismissed to the gymnasium where booths belonging to the parents of our students offered foods from all over the world. Kids had tickets to try these offerings. There was everything from baklava, to fried bananas, to ribs and fried chicken!! There was never any trouble that I can recall and they were always days to remember. Students were encouraged to report to school in their country's native clothing. Music from all over the world was being played all over the building. This day always made me cry.

'Frosty in da Hood'

Inner city school choirs are usually over the top. The majority of students, much like Whitney Houston and Jennifer Hudson, have a musical background rooted in their churches. The gospel element takes it over the top. After having seen the dress rehearsal of our Christmas production, I decided to invite my sister to the evening show. It is a show, I told her, that I would gladly pay to see. That evening we arrived early for this 7:30 show, which promptly commenced at 8:15. We were in the minority as two white women in this auditorium. My sister was in awe and a bit intimidated by the loud, late, seemingly unorganized nature of the production. The families, with loads of babies in tow, were streaming in. I was greeted and introduced to parents and babies alike. I remember being thankful that my sister witnessed the love and rapport that I enjoyed in my professional life.

Finally, the lights went down and the choir began to sing. I had been asked to hold a toddler while his mommy sang in the choir. As the choir rocked slowly back and forth, the baby spotted his mom on the risers, so near and yet so far, and he began to throw a fit. He became so disruptive that the choir director turned to me and motioned to let him go. This baby jumped from my lap, ran down the aisle, jumped into his mother's arms, and the choir never skipped a beat.

After a few awesome introductory numbers, a play was next: "Frosty in da Hood". Frosty entered the stage wearing a black do-rag. He was dancing around when, out of nowhere, appeared a gang of neighborhood thugs who attacked him and stole his do-rag. He pathetically melted to the ground without his magical head gear. All the sadness of the neighborhood was displayed by members of this worthy cast, until Sista Nature arrived, swirling through the curtains onto the stage, to save the day. She corralled the evil perpetrators and returned the magical do-rag to its rightful owner. Frosty immediately came alive and began to dance around the stage. It was hilarious and sweet and began our Christmas vacation in a huge way. My wonderful sister was in total culture shock, but thoroughly enjoyed the spectacle that it was.

"Scared Straight"

There were many "Scared Straight" programs coming to this school. One, in particular, made a huge impact on many of us. We were all in the gymnasium and were unaware of what we were about to witness. In walked four, chained together inmates. They were unchained and each, in turn, walked to the podium to tell his story. The story that had almost everyone in the audience crying was told by a skinny, sad, young man, who was serving a life sentence for murder. His story began with him revealing to us that while in high school, he was a nerd. He'd earned good grades and was never in trouble. He yearned to be in with the "in" crowd. He wanted to be wild. He wanted girls to notice him. One Friday he found himself invited to join a wild group of guys who would surely show him how to have a good time. They smoked weed. They drank. They were in a fast car. He didn't know whether to be afraid or to go with it. He went with it. They had a plan for that fateful night. Their plan was to rob a warehouse. His part in this foolproof plan was to drive the get-away car for them. Something went horribly wrong and a security guard was killed. All four boys were caught and charged with the same murder. All went down for life. His nerdy life was over. This was a lesson many were unaware of, in that if you are there, you are guilty. People must always be aware of the company they choose to keep. This one wild night changed everything for these boys, their families, and of course, the family of the dead security guard. All the nerds and the tough guys in the audience were in tears. This young man spoke of his grandmother and how he'd missed her funeral. He spoke of the fact that he'd never had sex and that he never would. He spoke of how being popular is so important to high schoolers and how seeking it can ruin lives.

Field Trips

I arranged for as many field trips as possible for my students. As I mentioned, many of these kids are from families that have no cars, let alone the means to travel. These kids depend upon their teachers to take them places. I noticed that even the toughest of the tough seemed intimidated and scared when they were out of their familiar element. Everyone wanted to hold my hand, sit next to me, and be the first one back on the bus. I took a large group of ninth and tenth graders to a local ice rink. Whenever it was possible, I would arrange to bring my son with us so he could have fun and play with these kids that were such a big part of my life. This was one of those times. Per usual, most of the kids had their own agendas. Many opted not to don skates, preferring to run around the ice in their shoes. They wanted to climb the mound of snow cleared by the Zamboni, make snow balls, and have snowball fights. My son was just in grade school at the time and was having the time of his life. He was particularly drawn to a boy by the name of Hassein They bonded and had a great time. Hassein served as my son's protector for that afternoon. Kenny often asked about Hassein following that day.

The school year went on and then came summer vacation. When school resumed in the fall, Hassein was not there. The news was that he was in prison for murdering his girlfriend's step-father by walking into their livingroom and shooting the man in the chest. His reason was that his girlfriend had shared with Hassein that her step-father was having sex with her. He "went off" and took the law into his own hands. I never knew if what the girlfriend had told him was true. I only know that I never saw Hassein again.

Another field trip I'd arranged for my students was to see "The Lion King". I was so thrilled and couldn't wait. I just knew they would love and appreciate this opportunity. This trip proved to be a bit of a disappointment for me though. Their behavior was less than respectful as far as I was concerned. I always threatened them with punishments that they never took seriously. I was sitting there thoroughly enjoying this marvelous play when I turned around to take a survey of my charges. Some were sleeping. Some were on their damn phones. Some were talking to each other. I was shocked and enraged. I grabbed phones and shook people awake and threatened never to take them anywhere with me ever again. They could not understand why I was "trippin".

I always loved doing plays with my students. One year we read "A Raisin in the Sun" by Lorraine Hansberry. We had such a great time acting it out for each other. The grandmother was played by Big Albert, one of the big boys who was not threatened by reading the part of an old black woman. He made it so much fun. I then showed them the movie starring Sidney Poitier. As luck would have it, the play was being presented at our downtown playhouse and I secured tickets. The day arrived and we all dressed up for this occasion. We all knew this play word for word. I informed those backstage that my class had just finished acting the play in our classroom. Following the play, the actors came out into the audience to meet my students! They gathered around us and spent time asking who played who. When they found that the grandmother was played by my Big Albert, they congratulated him and made him feel like a million bucks. That was truly a field trip to remember.

A trip to the local zoo was less than a perfect outing. When it came time to round everyone up and head toward the buses, some were at large and some were sick. The wildflowers who were sick, had broken into the shed that housed the primates' foods. They had eaten the bananas that were shot full of vitamins meant, of course, for the primates. These kids were violently ill, until all the primate vitamins were out of their systems. Needless to say, we were not invited to return to the zoo. I also had to stay behind, when the buses left, to locate the missing kids. One other teacher had driven his own car because he was arriving a bit late. We roamed around until we found our missing kids and returned to the school with our tails between our legs.

Shakespeare

While at this school, I presented my true love, Shakespeare, to my students. Like I mentioned before, if they like and trust you, there is nothing they won't do for you, including trying Shakespeare. "Romeo and Juliet" was on the syllabus. I first remember asking these kids if they trusted me. Of course they did and I told them they would like this. I let them know they would be reading a play that was much like a soap opera. It was about a little thirteen year old girl who was being stalked by an eighteen year old boy who had just broken up with another. It has lies, deceit, suicide, and murder. It turned out this story was right up their alley. Much to my surprise, they loved every minute of William Shakespeare's works. I went all out for the presentation. I loved Shakespeare and I wanted them to feel the same. When a teacher presents something he or she loves, it shows, and it rubs off. The enthusiasm is infectious.

We made banners with the names of all the characters boldly printed and hung them from our classroom ceiling. They were hung on one side of the room or the other, keeping the family members together and to show whose side each character was on for the students' convenience. We also prepared, with construction paper, name tags for these characters. Lamination was necessary to prevent the etchings of their various gang signs, which they could not restrain from doing. Each day, before they arrived, I would single out the laminated cards of those characters who would be covered that day. When the students arrived they fought over the cards and the readings for the day. Sometimes we would redo an act, just to spread the love allowing more than one person to give it a try. The class would then vote as to who they thought delivered a better, more believable, and professional rendition. It was absolutely amazing to watch. They did not hold back. Here's the key. Many,

many black kids are rappers. They think in terms of rhymes. They deliver with a beat. They are animated. They are not, for the most part, inhibited. They took to the language of Shakespeare like ducks to water.

There are five acts in every Shakespearean play. We went act by act, and then I showed them the movies, act by act, so they could compare their acting and deliveries to those of the pros. It was an incredible lesson plan that took many, many weeks. Those students who would sadly find themselves in trouble for which their punishment was a school suspension, would be sorely missed. Our secret classroom plan for these hard times was to send someone down to an outside door where the culprit would be let in secretly, just so he could participate in the reading of that day. No one wanted to miss out on even one act. I was in heaven.

We also conquered "Julius Caesar", "Macbeth", and finally "Othello". "Othello" was the best for me; it is a tragedy. In Shakespeare's tragedies, most all of the main characters wind up dead. This is a sad, frustrating story about an older black general who fell in love with, and married, a young blonde woman. They were absolutely in love, but as all good soap operas go, someone started a rumor that took on a life of its own. Jealousy and doubt invaded this perfect relationship until violence and death triumphed. Of course, it is all about power and greed started by one of Othello's jealous officers. Being that I was the only blonde in the class, I assumed the role of Desdemona. There were lots of scenes with lots of violence that we acted out over and over, trying to determine who performed the best. Proceeding act by act, as usual, we took our time with this play. After they read the play and saw the movie, in which Lawrence Fishburne played Othello, I then showed the classes the newer, updated version, called "O". This I came upon by accident. This movie was about a black college basketball star and his white college cheerleader girlfriend. This was perfection for ending what was that last time I would present a Shakespearean play before my retirement. These were some of my finest moments.

"The Crucible"

There were a couple other "finest moments" in my career. One was the presentation of "The Crucible", and the other was John Steinbeck's "The Pearl". Like I mentioned before, the enthusiasm of the teacher is infectious. If you happen to like and find a written work of art to be valuable in the lessons it can teach, it will show. Introducing "The Crucible" was easy. I obtained the movie and let them see the first scene only. The first scene shows all the town's young girls sneaking one night out of their bedroom windows and down ladders to meet in the woods to dance, which was strictly prohibited . . . . and then I turned it off! Also, as introduction, I asked them just exactly what each and every one of them would do in order to avoid a beating. We all agreed that a lie would be the least of what they would do to avoid a beating. We also determined that parents who beat their children will absolutely create good liars out of their children in order to avoid these beatings. This is exactly what the girls in this play did; they lied.

I also presented "The Crucible" as a play about a woman scorned. The star character in this play did what she did because of a man's rejection of her. She thought he loved her. He didn't. Can you imagine how this plot took hold of my wildflowers? They all had their own stories. They all could identify at some point, with some character, while reading this play. It too was incredible to behold. The mob mentality that took over was particularly gripping and educational for these kids. The power of a rumor was revealed and discussed at length. Rumors were at the bottom of many a fight taking place in our halls. Somebody's gay. Somebody's cheating on somebody. Somebody stole something. Somebody's pregnant. Somebody's had an abortion. Somebody's mama's a whore. Somebody's daddy's in jail. Somebody's homeless. This play also had parts the students wanted to act out over and over again. We had so much fun. Every time a class has fun, more bonding takes place.

"Roots"

There were several years where I was given the task of teaching "Black History" to my juniors. These kids already knew me and when I announced this to them, we all had a good laugh. I told them there was nothing I wouldn't try and we could learn together. "Roots" by Alex Haley immediately came to my mind. "Roots" was released as a mini-series in 1977. I remember this specifically because I was pregnant during this time and it made a huge impression on me. Many of these students' parents weren't even aware of this book or movie. I felt it was so important that I arranged to show it in its entirety over the course of six weeks. My plan was to show a tape, of which there were six, every Friday. Being on the block schedule of ninety minute class periods, gave us enough time to do so. After viewing, we would talk a bit about what we saw and their weekend assignment was to write a paper as a response due to me on Monday. The students were so invested in this project that they looked forward to our Fridays. Some even brought their parents who were following the story with their kids through their papers. Everyone should see this movie. It is an American must. Their papers were so heartfelt and honest that I looked forward to their opinions and their views as they stated them in these very candid papers. Some shared their papers with the class. I corrected and edited these masterpieces for them to re-write until they were perfect and ready for display on the walls of our classroom.

I had every scene of this movie memorized and knew what to expect as far as their emotional reactions. Some of my pregnant girls had understandable overt reactions to the treatment of mothers and their babies and children and how they were separated at the callous will of the plantation owners. I would position myself among these girls with tissues necessary for the viewing or for the girl who had to leave the room. This was yet another very rewarding unit that I completely enjoyed with my wildflowers.

Jury Duty

This was a class of juniors that I just simply adored. There were good kids, bad kids, rappers, gay kids, a cross dresser, athletes, cheerleaders, nerds . . . . and me. We loved each other so much that if anyone was absent, it just wasn't the same. We needed everyone present in order to be complete. I was called to jury duty and required to make arrangements for ten working days! That's a lifetime, a lifetime of lesson plans, and a lifetime of worrying. I worried about what they would do to my room. I worried about what they would do to my momentum. But, most of all, I worried about the sub. Substitutes are targets. The mission of the day was to make the sub cry, or leave, or both. The day I announced I would be gone for so long, I asked them if they would please be good. The answer was a resounding, "No! We are going to be bad until you get back here!" And they meant it. When I returned after what seemed like forever, they were ecstatic and full of complaints about how they had been abused by their subs. I was sympathetic and played along with them. They knew darn well that I knew what had taken place. They had systematically driven out three substitutes, who left without notice, by way of the closest stairwell available, saying there was no amount of money in the world that was worth this abuse. These were juniors whom I had in the palm of my hand. Somehow this gave me a sense of pride. They loved me and no one was about to take my place.

For those of us who have done our civic duty and served on a jury, we know it is a long, screening process to seat twelve jurors and one alternate. I happened to be dating a local police officer at the time and revealed this when asked about my affiliations. The judge asked me about stories this police officer may share with me and about how I would react and handle these stories. To this I simply said that because of where I work, I have much better stories than he does. The entire room exploded in laughter and I was seated to serve on this jury.

It was with these juniors that I enjoyed joking, to the point of becoming a bit politically incorrect. A few girls often left the noise of the cafeteria to dine with me in the privacy of my classroom. They were wonderful young ladies who all three enjoyed extreme popularity and always knew how to have fun. It was the day before Christmas vacation. We had secretly agreed to have a private gift exchange. The three were heading toward my room, all dressed in red, wearing Santa hats. I called down the hallway that they so got me into the Christmas spirit and pointing to each one I yelled, "Hoe! Hoe! Hoe!" Not many people could get away with that!

These ladies have returned to our building to visit me after their graduations. They say whenever they think of me they think of my yelling, "Hoe! Hoe! Hoe!" down the hall at them!

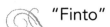

"Finto"

I laughed myself sick over this incident with a ninth grade girl, who was a great sport about the whole thing. Whenever I gave a written assignment, I always read and graded everything with care. After sometimes several re-writes, the final product was to be hung in the room for all to admire. I always wrote something personal as my response to the author, in hopes of starting some sort of dialogue. Most looked forward to my comments and it was our own personal conversation. If time allowed, I'd be able to read and grade a paper while sitting with the student. On this particular occasion the class was engaged in an assignment when Angelique had her paper ready to turn in, just a little late. We were reading together when we came to a word that was foreign to me . . . . "finto". I looked at her and asked, "What's 'finto'?" She looked at me like I was crazy and responded, "Ya know, 'finto'." Like ya 'finto' go to work, or ya 'finto' go to the store!" I fell apart when the light bulb went off for me. Kids write the way they talk!

Teacher assaults

"One man's trash is another man's treasure" is a quote that comes to my mind with regard to students. No one can like everyone. No one can relate to everyone, and the behavior of a particular student in one teacher's classroom is never the behavior displayed in the next. People respond differently toward different people. Kids even relate differently to their two parents. This is my introduction to talking about teacher assaults. I have my own educated theory about teacher assaults. Throughout my career I've watched patterns develop. It was very interesting to witness all of the attention the "victim" would receive, and all the trouble in which the perpetrator would find himself. It seemed to always be the same teachers. When one is assaulted, one is entitled to a ten day paid vacation and lots of sympathy from his or her peers, while the perp is arrested and does some time downtown, with assault on his or her record. One female teacher comes to my mind. She was a woman who truly disliked our students, if not all kids. She was always talking down to them, not only to other teachers, but to their faces. I saw her try to humiliate, and put students in impossible situations. She would back a pissed off kid into a corner and berate and scream, until . . . he or she would fight his or her way out of that corner. This seems to be common sense that one should never corner someone who is already raging. This is a guaranteed assault and subsequent ten day vacation. It was very much a set up for the kid. She knew that she would be the winner. I witnessed her do this several times. I hated her for it and said within earshot of her that I could work for a thousand years and never be assaulted once. There are ways of dealing with people and hers was not the way it was done.

A male teacher in another building displayed the very same behaviors and was out on assault leave a couple times a year. He too would corner a pissed off kid and be oh so shocked when he would be pushed out of the way. These people used to play the victim card to the point where they would make me want to throw up.

A personal friend relayed his sad story of his untimely exodus from high school. It was a science teacher who cornered him. Tom warned the guy more than once not to touch him. The teacher didn't heed this warning and the two male egos were unleashed. The man pushed the kid. The kid fought back. The teacher ended up on the floor and the student was arrested. Tom was ultimately expelled from school. He was seventeen years old and his first thought was to join the marines and go to Viet Nam. His life was forever changed, as all who served in that war were changed. He's had broken marriages and a severe drinking and drug problem following his Viet Nam days. If that teacher had just stepped back and let the pissed off kid calm down, I wonder where Tom would be today. Egos got in the way. How humiliating for both sides to have been the loser in the eyes of the rest of the class. A good teacher has to know when to say when. If one keeps the best interest of the child foremost in one's mind, I don't see how anyone can lose.

Of course I am not condoning violence, and there are teachers who are completely innocent that are assaulted, however, the key is if it keeps happening over and over, something should be done about that teacher.

My failure

I have to admit of a complete failure on my part to connect with one young girl. This girl hated me, and no matter how I tried, she continued to hate me. She arrived new to the class with a huge chip on her shoulder. She was absolutely beautiful. She was a light skinned black girl with 'good hair'. She was the most argumentative, nasty, hateful, young girl I had come across in a very long time. She was not only mean to me, she was mean to her peers. I'd arranged for a mediation with our principal, thinking that of course, I could melt her down with kindness. I obtained some background on this girl through the principal, with whom I was good friends. She was being raised by her lesbian mother and a series of her mother's partners. She was having a very hard time adjusting to this home situation and had had some bad experiences with previous partners. My heart went out to her and I thought that my loving kindness would win her over. She did not budge. She dug her heels in even harder and was unrelenting. We ended the mediation agreeing to disagree.

The next episode that arose with this girl was that of catching her cheating. She was completely guilty and was asked to leave the room and go to the principal, because I was unable to deal with her. She refused to go and chose to cause a huge scene. Security was called in and she stormed out. What she did when she stormed out was call her mother, who obviously was not far from the school because she showed up unannounced and rushed into my classroom wanting a confrontation with me. The protocol for a visit is to go through the office, which she did not do. Her daughter entered the classroom right behind her, smiling, waiting for her mom to kick my ass right in front of everybody. I stood from the student desk I was seated in at the front of the class and swung the desk around in front of me. She charged at me when the security guards showed up. She was escorted out in handcuffs. I turned to my class and asked the boys sitting in the front if they were going to let that happen. Two of them were members of our football team and could have over-powered her. They assured me that they were not going to let it happen, that they had my back. The kids seemed to take this whole thing in stride, but I was scared out of my mind. This was a woman who looked like a man and was the size of a man and she was pissed at me for picking on her daughter. I was not going to win with this girl and I was now done trying. Arrangements were made to have her placed with another English teacher. It was reported that she bonded immediately with this black teacher and my problems with her were over.

Taking the fights in stride was exactly what they did. The adults around them were always involved in some sort of drama. No one seems to care that the kids are watching and remembering. I was packing and preparing for Christmas vacation. A young man stopped by my room to say his good-byes and to wish me a merry Christmas. When I asked what his family had planned for the holidays his response was that it never really mattered what was planned, that his older sisters and his aunties always drink too much and get into such loud awful fights that spill out into the street that the police are usually summoned. He said it was the same story every holiday and because of this he hates holidays and wasn't even happy about the break from school.

I recall a fight for which my whole third floor classroom and I had the best seats in the house. We were in a very old brick building that had steam heating and it was warm enough all winter that we sometimes opened our huge windows. We heard yelling and cussing from down below. It was two girls who were fighting over God knows what. Then their mamas enter the scene, both tearing off their shirts, both revealing their red bras, to no doubt demonstrate to their daughters how real women take care of business. The whole school was watching, at least those on that side of the building. It was the most ridiculous display of juvenile behavior by all four females. I felt embarrassed for the girls witnessing their mothers act in such a way, or sadly perhaps this was their norm?

There were a few wildflowers that we teachers worried about when we had vacations or long weekends. It was observed that some would return having lost weight. It is true what they say about hunger in America; there are definitely hungry kids in our schools. They absolutely come to school for the meals.

Breathe with me

One technique I found to be helpful was breathing through a temper tantrum with the student. I shared with my classes that I had a secret way of calming kids down. First of all, they were curious. They would admit that tantrums are not fun. Feeling like one may explode is awful, and if I could suggest to them a way to avoid that feeling, they were willing to listen and try it. Kids would leave a class, leave the cafeteria, leave the gym, and make their way to my class when they felt something coming on. The urge to throw something, hurt someone, or kill someone was often the motivation. When I saw a student at my door in obvious distress, I would excuse myself from the class and out in the hallway, I would grab both hands and say, "Breathe with me, Girl/Boy". I'd previously taught them that forcing air into our brains had a calming effect on the human body. We would sometimes breathe for quite a while until hands were ready to be released. Then the tears would start and the hugs were needed. The awaiting class always knew someone was in need and never became a problem. The student would never become a target, because as I told them, you never know when it will be your turn. My goal with this was for them to eventually be able to calm themselves down, no matter where they were.

Many teenagers have been enrolled in some court mandated anger management program. When I would inquire as to how it was going for them, many would tell me how it just made them madder! The key to success with teens is that they must like and trust you or they won't hear a word you say. I am not saying I could calm everyone down. That would be ridiculous, however, my successes were many and rewarding.

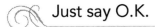 Just say O.K.

I also had some advice for my classes that I learned from my son, and his dealings with me. My son and I had some very rough times during his high school years. I was always "on his back" for things that I would now let go. It was a matter of learning to choose my battles wisely. The way this savvy teenager dealt with me was to just say "O.K." to anything I'd ask of him. It didn't matter what he intended to do afterwards, he said, "O.K". Who could argue with that? A fight never got off the ground. When I shared this tactic with my students, I had more than one happy kid tell me that it worked for him too. Let's face it, parents and teens don't see eye to eye and the parents aren't always right, however they have the power. This can be very frustrating for any kid. Stopping any confrontation is always a good thing. Just say "O.K".

Curtis

Curtis was one of a set of twins who took turns coming in and out of the detention center. Both boys were enrolled in yet another "special program" for "at risk" students. Four teachers who had volunteered for this program and our students were isolated from the rest of the school, off to one end of the basement. I was approaching our area when I saw a mass of people at the base of a staircase. I heard the word "gun". I heard the word "Curtis". I probably would not react today the same way as I did that day, however, I plowed through that crowd, got face to face with Curtis and said, "Give me that gun and come with me!" He did. The crowd parted and let us walk out hand in hand up to the office with the gun in my hand. The boy was short and very stocky and strong, because every time he got locked up, all he did was hit the weights and bulk up. He was his own worst enemy and was obviously glad to have this event interrupted, because he let me be the hero . . . thank God. I knew this boy. I knew he would not hurt me, however, I do realize how naïve I was, but this was also back in the eighties, when school shootings were not what they are today.

My students and I analyzed these events that are all over the news these days. What they recognized right away is that it was never a black kid! It seems usually to be nerdy, white kids who have had a vendetta against a bully. They saw that the pattern was for the retaliation to take place after months of planning, plotting, mapping, and strategizing for the target date. They said that black kids take care of it on the spot. Immediate gratification at its worst.

Chapter 7

Working in the Slammer

In spite of how wonderful a school is, and in spite of the long list of priceless memories being made within its walls, time marches on and things change, and all good things must come to an end. Within this huge metropolitan arena, the powers that be deemed it time to close my school. To me and many others it was an end of an era. We marched and protested and wrote petitions, all to no avail. It closed. The entire staff had to be re-assigned. We were allowed our three top choices of the schools to which we would prefer reassignment. While in a checkout line in a corner drug store, I ran into a friend who was teaching at the county juvenile detention center down town. That sounded like it was right up my alley. I had no idea such a school even existed, but even our incarcerated juvenile population is entitled to an education, like it or not.

I wanted to be wise about my choices, so I took a couple sick days in order to visit this facility. I was led through six locked doors, and arrived on the third floor where the inmates were schooled. The hallway was lined with locked classroom doors. Across the hallway from the classrooms were the social workers' offices. The principal's office was at one end and the teachers' bathroom at the other. There were bars on the windows. The boys were kept separate from the girls. Everyone was dressed in jailhouse blue uniforms and were silently led to their classrooms in single file with their hands behind their backs. The classrooms were small and there were usually no more than fifteen students per classroom. I remember feeling very sad for these kids. There were those wildflowers who said it wasn't so bad being locked up. This speaks volumes as to the lives they led on the outside. You might say these are the kids whose pictures are on no one's dressers. They spoke of their "three hots and a cot" living arrangement. Some claimed to even like the food. At least while they were incarcerated they were assured of their three meals and a warm single bed to sleep on every night. For many, this was a definite improvement. I remember wondering what went wrong in their lives that led them to this jackpot. I also remember thinking that if they had had me for a mom they would not be in this situation. Most of the teaching staff were middle aged white women. I learned from them that discipline was not an issue for obvious reasons; they were anxious to get out of their cells. They were bored and welcomed something to do. The teachers were nice to them. The inmates were under the impression that the teachers had hot lines to their judges and they were eager to make good impressions on us teachers.

I was granted this assignment, but only after a teacher with more seniority bid for it and got it first. She, however, did not do her homework and visit the facility beforehand. It was very early on that she realized that she could not deal with the closed conditions. She felt anxious and claustrophobic every day. She couldn't get used to the musty smell of the kids. She couldn't deal with the depths of depression the students were living with on a daily basis. Due to the business of the red tape, the switch was made after six weeks. I loved it so much. I really felt I was making a difference. It was unlike anything I'd ever experienced. There was always someone crying. There was an enormous amount of depression. Kids were taken from classrooms and escorted to courtrooms. Sometimes they returned. Sometimes they left immediately to serve their sentences elsewhere. There were a huge number of repeat offenders. If a teacher was there long enough, he or she knew everyone. Some kids were even known to have "grown up" there. There were a lot of family members incarcerated at one time. Some families regard incarceration as a rite of passage into adulthood.

At the end of the school day, all the teachers would leave together. On our way out we would pass those entering to visit their children. The choking smell of alcohol, marijuana, and body odor was sometimes overwhelming. These kids were, for the most part, born into such defeated circumstances that where they were now was no surprise. I felt badly for those who had no visitors. One boy complained to me that he was so disappointed in his mama because she never visited him. He revealed to me all of the gifts he'd bestowed upon her with his illegally gotten money, and now she wouldn't even visit him. He was a crier.

The stories from the "slammer"' are never ending for me. The telling of these stories is where I heard most often that I should write a book. I was there for five years. Something notable happened every day. Some are funny. Some would rip your heart out. Some are one-liners. Some could be a book all its own. Some, you'd have had to have been there, others would entertain the masses. As they entered the classrooms, they placed their I.D. cards on the teacher's desk. They would take their seats and wait for class to begin. When I started teaching there, the boys wore two piece outfits, the pants having an elastic waist. I soon noticed that many, many of these boys sat with their hands down their pants. I asked one of the correction officers what that was all about. He looked at me, and his simple answer was, "Cuz it feels good". Within a couple of years these two piece outfits were replaced by jumpsuits with no easy access to the feel good region. Reading the names of these wildflowers is an acquired talent. It is not the last names that pose the problems, it is the uniquely made-up first names. I became surprising adept at pronouncing them correctly the first time. This, alone, earned me some respect. One boy's card read, "Alpacino" as his first name. I asked him what he wanted to be called. He looked at me like I was crazy and said, "Alpacino, Girl. Why you trippin'?"

I had the pleasure of meeting a Vincent Price, a SirJuan, a Lord, a Sincere, sets of twins named Jonathan and Shawnathon, Cedrik and Dedrik, three sisters named Beautiful, Wonderful, and Treasure, and two girls with the name of Holly Wood. Of course there were a couple girls named Precious. One Precious was a teenage dancer at night. She was one of the roughest girls I'd ever seen in my life and she looked much older than her sixteen years. I happened to be within a stone's throw of one of Precious's meltdowns. She was put in handcuffs in front of her body instead of in back. She went wild and literally broke the cuffs apart! Everyone, including me, jumped to restrain this girl. I was sitting on her forearm, while others were sitting on the three other limbs. It was like restraining a wild animal that had unbelievable strength. Anyway, I digress. Back to the uniqueness of names. My personal explanation as to why the first names are so unique goes back to slave days, where the plantation owners used to rename, at will, and the last names were, of course, that of the owner. Maybe the young mothers don't even know where this practice comes from, however, one could walk into any city school and ask for a child using just the first name.

As a rookie, I was not afraid. I was there to help and lend some understanding and possibly some knowledge. The classes were small for obvious reasons. They always wanted to talk. I would ask for a show of hands of those who had been framed. They all would raise their hands! They were all so very sorry, but I soon learned that most were so very sorry . . . that they had been caught! The complaints were many, from the treatment they received from the correction officers, to the soap they referred to as "car wash soap". One pitiful young man held back a bit from the rest as they were leaving my classroom to show me the rash that this "car wash soap" had caused. He asked me if I could please bring him some decent soap and that he would not tell any of the others. That night I thought about it and couldn't come up with a reason why I shouldn't. I brought in a bar of Ivory soap for this kid. He was thrilled when I presented it to him on the down low. I was so proud of myself for being such a kind hearted woman.

The very next day, walking in the building, and passing through the six locked doors to get to the teaching floor, something was not right. There was an alarm sounding and lights were flashing, all of which was new to me. The problem was this: Some prisoner had jammed the doors with bar soap so as to prevent them from locking! How could this be? He was such a sweet kid! I had to come clean and reveal my rookie, silly, white woman stupidity. To my great shock, I was not fired. They let it go with a warning to never trust an inmate or question the rules. These kids are here for a reason, and all they want to do is escape. I felt foolish and learned a valuable lesson, for if this was where I was going to be teaching for a while, I'd better wise up.

I was informed of another trick the inmates had been known to try, of coercing the teacher to bring in candy. In schools on the outside lots of teachers use candy as a bargaining tool. In the slammer one is unaware of who may be a diabetic. A diabetic might eat the candy to intentionally cause a diabetic reaction, to be rushed to the hospital, which was across the street, to plot his escape from there. These wildflowers were always thinking about escaping.

The desperation of their lives, we free, law-abiding citizens could never imagine. From running the streets at will and being completely on his own, an inmate was now reduced to asking for toilet paper, lining up for everything from a shower, to food, to classes. It was a complete role reversal for these "Alpha dog'" personalities. For those who could not or would not read or write, the days were long and boring. Planning fights and planning escapes had to be primary on their dream lists.

A seventeen year old Puerto Rican boy placed a folded piece of paper in my hand as he was exiting my classroom. This is what he wrote: "I got $18,000 and a Katawa Suzuki '97' motorcycle. Get me out and its yours . . . all of it!" and he signed his name! This is yet another piece of memorabilia that I have framed and hung in my kitchen. This poor boy mistook my kindness for weakness for sure. This boy was incarcerated for having killed a man for his car. He was headed for a very long stay behind bars.

The next day I told him I was flattered by his trust in me, however, there would be no way I would jeopardize my career. I told him I would take it no farther and that we need never speak of it again.

The kids were taken right from our classrooms and escorted to court. The teachers were all asked to write reports for the judges regarding the behavior in class of every student for his or her court appearances. Like I mentioned, every kid was eager to leave his cell and come to school. They were anxious to do something, anything, and they knew we wrote to their judges. As a result, they were usually pretty good and cooperative in our classes. My reports were usually on the positive side, however, I would include in my report to the judge that this did not mean I would recommend he or she be released to live next door to me! One little guy was a nervous wreck awaiting his escort to court. After being gone only a very short while, he was returned to my classroom and slammed himself down in his seat. We all were very anxious to hear what in the world had happened. All he could tell us through his temper was

1 gt 18,000 + a 750 KAHAWA
ZUZUKI "97"
MOTOR CYCLE

get me out and is yours
all of it

Rafael Martinez

that his lawyer made him "Flea bargain!" This young man had no idea what was going on.

Another crazy, bad, little boy who was always in some sort of trouble within the walls of the detention center was escorted from my classroom to his day in court. I remember this kid was annoying and extremely immature. He even irritated his peers. He too was returned to my classroom after court and was not at all happy. He told the class that the judge said that he needed to spend more time locked up until more testing could be administered. He asked me what I thought of that. I responded with a very honest answer that I did indeed think that he was difficult. At that, he jumped up from his seat, throwing his chair backwards. He ran to my desk and cleared it off with one fell swoop. He ran to the book shelves, clearing them to the ground as well. This all went down in a matter of seconds. The rest of the small class just watched in utter amazement. When he was done, he plopped back down in his seat, winded, leaned over to the older guy next to him and asked, "What do difficult mean?"

This calm older classmate simply looked at the crazy, and said, "You tear the lady room up and you don't even know what difficult mean?"

The arsonist

The youngest inmate, let alone the youngest student, I'd ever encountered, was a ten year old arsonist. The easiest weapon for a ten year old to get his hands on may not be a gun or a knife or a bomb, but he can always find a match. According to the social worker in charge of this child, he was the son of a prostitute. When business came her way, she would put her son out to roam the streets in the wee hours. Random fires were set, until he was apprehended and placed in our juvenile detention center. He was a fighter; he would lunge at other students, lunge at correction officers, or whomever got in his path. It mattered not that he would never be the winner due to his size and age. He was like a wild animal always on the attack. It was determined that he had to be isolated, in a class all by himself and I was the lucky teacher. He would not lunge at me for some reason. I read to him, talked to him, let him sleep, and did some serious bonding. The correction officers brought in stuffed animals for his cell. Social workers brought blankets. He was ten. He was a mess. It was not his fault. Another case of faulty parenting. During one of our talks I asked him if he had a hero. He said his hero was his grandfather. "My grandpa. He's dead now. He was a baller." His grandfather was probably in his thirties. A "baller" is someone who always has money. I would imagine his "baller" granddad was probably involved, in some way, with drugs, and died at an early age due to his lifestyle. The boy splashed real tears over his deceased grandfather. The man was probably the only person in the boy's life who made him feel wanted and loved; his mother certainly didn't. Another question I asked him was if he could recall the best time of his life. He thought and thought and came up with, "I once went to a pizza party". This broke my heart. At ten, this boy's fondest memory was that of a pizza party. After school that day I stopped at a grocery store. In the lunch section, I located and bought the Lunchable brand pizzas. It consisted of all the necessary ingredients for little individual homemade pizzas. The next day he and I had our own little pizza party. With his grubby little hands, he put together the best little pizzas one could ever imagine . . . . and he offered the first one to me!

The issues this little guy was dealing with, most of us could never grasp. He was his own worst enemy and was hell bent on fighting the entire world. More than once, loud disturbances were due to our little arsonist on the attack. More than once, I was summoned to see if I could be a calming force, however, once he was on a roll, there really was no stopping him. It was almost like he had to wear himself out before he could stop. After such an event, he would sleep for hours, almost like the aftermath of an epileptic seizure. Unless some super-sized mental health intervention was administered, which was highly unlikely, there seemed very little hope that he would ever lead a happy, and productive life on the outside. Thanks Mom.

High profile

Just like in the adult prisons, the inmates are allowed to watch television. They too are aware of the crimes being committed and who is going where. When high profile convicts, like Susan Smith, Scott Peterson, and Casey Anthony are placed, I often wonder how they are treated by their peers. No one likes child killers, or women abusers. Some have to be moved and some must be kept in isolation. There were a couple of high profile juveniles who were soon to be placed with us. Roman was the fourteen year old father and Blondie was the sixteen year old mother of a one year old child they were charged with killing. It was said that these kids were living in a known crack house. A crack house is no place for a teenager, let alone a toddler, or anyone for that matter, but children have little or no choices or power over their circumstances. It was said that someone, in his or her stupor, rolled over on and smothered this baby. Knowing we were to be admitting this fourteen year old father, everyone was curious, especially the kids. When he walked in, surprisingly enough, he was your very average, skinny, little fourteen year old boy. He was quiet and looked lost and scared. I never got to talk with him or develop any kind of an opinion about him, because that night he was severely beaten by his peers and when he was released from the hospital, he was taken to be housed in another county's juvenile detention center for his own safety.

Blondie was another story. She was a large, black girl, with blonde hair. She was so upbeat and fun-loving, you'd think she didn't have a care in the world. Her baby boy was dead and she was being charged. She was seemingly unaware and uncaring as to the turn her life was about to take. She too was shipped out after the first day to be relocated into the adult system, due to the gravity of her crime. Just think about how unimportant it seemed her son was to her. If you continue thinking about it, you may just conclude how unimportant Blondie might have been to those who raised her. She seemed to be missing the "sympathy" and "empathy" part of her personality. I never did get an update on these two unfortunate individuals, however, once again, if I were their mother, they would not have been raised in a crack house. No good can ever come from inside the walls of a crack house. At the very least, homework would never be the priority. Their baby never had a chance.

Baby Huey

Another high profile case was that of an elementary school principal who was having a sexual relationship with one of her sixth grade boys. It must be explained that a school, any school, is much like a city and the principal is the highest governing force. The principal is usually the most highly educated, the most highly paid, and the most feared and revered member of the school family.

Her victim was expected in our facility due to drug charges. Putting an actual face with the name and the crime made it so real. We were all so curious as to what this young boy would look like. Also, always high profile, is the large number of teachers who have crossed the line with their students. As teachers, we've all had students whose attractive looks we could admire and know that one day he or she would grow to become a beautiful or handsome adult. Sadly, some cross that line, but most of us regard kids as kids. Some youngsters mature faster than others, with facial hair, bone structure, and body types. Upon learning of this boy having a sexual relationship with this grown woman, we all expected he would be one of those kids. We were all shocked to the core to see this tall, lumbering, plump boy who walked in with his thumb in his mouth. I knick-named him "Baby Huey". His teeth were misshapen and literally formed around that thumb of his. He caressed his nose as he sucked. He was a six foot tall mystery. There was nothing mature or attractive about this twelve year old boy. What perverse sexual behaviors went on between this woman and this child? What did she teach him? What did she have him do? What was her motivation? How did she make this poor soul feel at the tender age of twelve? I remember the way she looked in the courtroom. She was a matronly, homely, middle-aged white woman, who simply had the power. Who would have believed this boy at the onset? She was a predator in every sense of the word. Shame on her.

The story began with the principal taking this boy under her wing due to the information she had regarding this child's unfortunate home life. Predators prey on the most vulnerable and she certainly preyed upon him. The long term ramifications on this victim's psyche are insurmountable. The path of his life, which wasn't great to begin with, was forever altered. She changed who he could have and would have become. She began taking him home with her. She gave him money. He latched on to her as his "Sugar Mama", and so did his older brother, and his brother's girlfriend, and the boys' mother. The brother, the girlfriend, and the boy eventually moved into the principal's home. She took the whole family to Disney World. She bought the mother a Cadillac. She began doing the drugs that were being sold from her home. This woman had lost her mind. The mother was blackmailing this principal, and allowing her to continue this sick and twisted relationship with her twelve year old son. There was violence in the home due to the brother's drug business. It was said that she'd become a "crackhead".

This sensational trial was caught on the news. The female judge told the mother that her mothering was no better than that of a dog, and that it was very clear that she was allowing this abuse to continue while profiting handsomely from it. We all witnessed the mother lose control in the courtroom. She was writhing around on the courtroom floor, screaming about the injustice of it all. The principal continued to profess her love for this little boy she'd victimized. Both women were given very harsh sentences. They would be behind bars for a very long time. The brother and his girlfriend were charged with drug trafficking and prostitution. The twelve year old was charged with drug trafficking as a minor.

This poor little boy was raised in a hurricane of mistreatment and he'd become used to it. Happy people were a mystery to him. His mom was in prison. His brother was in prison. His "Sugar Mama" was in prison. When he was released, I'm sure he was enrolled in the never-ending cycle of foster care. At eighteen, he'd be released from the government books and left to his own devices. I never knew what became of "Baby Huey".

I do, however, recall a day when "Baby Huey" was leaving my classroom, at the end of the line, with his hands behind his back, as all the young inmates were required to do while traveling through the detention center. I was always "Ms. Suzi Sunshine", trying to be a positive light in their otherwise dismal days. They all knew I was happy to see them and they could regard my oasis as a soft place to fall. He looked at me and said, "You smile so much. It's almost like you never had anything bad happen to you in your whole life." Compared to his life, I hadn't.

They know not what they do

A fifteen year old girl in my class who was quite pregnant, was quite verbal about her plight and was sharing her search for the perfect name. I always asked the kids if they would ever consider naming a little girl after me . . . Judy. They all laughed and said it was such an "old school" sounding name, and that I just had to be trippin'. This little girl knew she was having a little girl and loved the sound of a word she'd heard. The word was chlamydia! Oh my God! She had no idea in the world what the word meant, and neither did anyone else in the room. They seemed to agree that it was a sweet sounding word. Needless to say, she had to remain with me after class to learn the meaning of the word and that it was certainly not what she would ever want to name her innocent little baby girl.

The crimes committed by these wildflowers were anything and everything from drug related charges to murder. One sweet little girl who could have starred as one of the Cosby kids was in for stabbing her mother to death. She dragged her murdered mom down to their basement and then called her in sick to her job for days, until she was discovered. Perhaps one's first reaction is to be horrified by this deed, until you realize how awful her mother must have been to draw such a brutal reaction from her fourteen year old daughter. Not everyone is blessed with the "Kool-aid mom" of the neighborhood. I never knew the details, however, I doubt that the girl just struck out over nothing.

There was another fourteen year old girl who had killed her stalker ex-boyfriend. Due to the grandparents of this boy coming forward to confirm this girl's accusations, her sentence, as well as the sentence of the aforementioned girl, was to serve until the age of twenty-one, then be released.

Kimba was a large, crazy-looking, older boy who was in for murdering his pizza delivery man. He had the biggest and messiest Afro I'd ever seen. He was feared and left alone by all. Upon learning of this dastardly deed, I promptly demanded that my son quit his pizza delivery job and look for something else. I told him that if he needed money that badly, I'd give it to him!

 ## Sex crimes

As is the truth throughout America's prison system, the largest percentage of inmates in the detention center are black. It can be a pretty frightening environment for your average white kid, when he finds himself among such a cast of characters. Three, clean-cut, white teenagers were escorted onto the unit. When I found they were residents of an affluent suburb near me, I felt a bit sorry for them. Ray Charles could have seen how terrified these boys were. My unsolicited advice to these three was to try to look crazy. Do your best Jeffrey Dahmer impressions and no one will bother you. Try to make your eyes look wild. Twitch. Maybe mumble to yourselves. You will be left alone because nobody likes "crazy". They adhered to my advice and no one bothered them.

This was a case where I wished I'd withheld my unsolicited advice. I learned from the social workers of their crimes. These boys had been arrested for participating in a gang rape! How sweet! I would have wanted them to encounter helplessness, hopelessness, and fear. Maybe a dose of reality would have served them well, rather than receiving advice from me on how they could avoid it all. Shame on me and yet another lesson learned.

Another sex crime committed by a skinny, white boy from the burbs made the papers. This was in the early years of on-line crimes. It was felt that an example had to be made of this crime. This boy knowingly sent a would-be adult predator to his bully's home address. This young internet criminal's wealthy parents (who probably prided themselves on providing the latest technology for their son) made heartfelt pleas to their lawyer, the judge, the newspapers, and anyone else who would listen, but his sentence was the harshest it could have been. He was a ninth grader, who looked like a sixth grader, whose maximum sentence was to be served in a maximum security prison for sex offending juveniles. He was to remain there until his twenty-first birthday. The judge was not going to let these rich, white parents, with their fancy lawyer, get away with anything less.

 ## Snitches get stitches

Attitude is everything, they say. There is a saying among thieves that "Snitches get stitches". Rico had been incarcerated on drug related charges for a very long time, awaiting his trial and sentencing. He made it known that a "friend" had snitched on him and that was why he'd been caught. His day in court arrived and to everyone's delight, the judge chose to release him, due to his good behavior and the fact that it had been his first offense. He was sitting in his social worker's office, which was across the hall from my classroom, signing his release papers and receiving a little pep talk from her. I stuck my head in to wish him well and to say I didn't want to see him come back. We hugged and the day went on.

The very next day, as I was unlocking my classroom door and I saw Rico sitting with his social worker. He was staring into space and she was crying. The first thing Rico did with his freedom was track down his "snitch" and kill him. He was now incarcerated on a murder charge. All I could say was, "I guess you showed him".

 ## Ignorance is bliss

Working in the slammer put an end to my desire to watch the news or to read the newspapers. All too often I would recognize a student from the back of his head, of course. Sometimes knowing of their crimes was not such a good thing when I needed to remain impartial and unbiased for simple classroom purposes. Antoine was one of the older boys. He was a gifted rapper and writer. He spent his bunk time, alone, writing raps and would present them to the class. He was totally entertaining and brilliant. His raps were of his life, his family, his girlfriend, and his son. His raps were sad. I learned to listen to and respect the lyrics of these products. He even wrote a rap about me and my classes.

While watching the news, I recognized the back of Antoine's neck and head and learned of his crime. He had leaped over the counter of a Seven-Eleven, and put a bullet in the head of a clerk, who was a young mother of three. Her family attended court as did his family. I was in shock that this was the talented young man with whom I engaged every single day. The next morning when I saw him, I told him I'd seen him on the news. He said, "I'm sorry you had to see that. Now you know where my words come from. I hate myself." He shared with me and the class his cautionary tale of that fateful night that he wished he would have listened to his mama and his baby's mama when they begged him to stay home and play cards with them. They told him they had a bad feeling about that night. He made the gangsta decision to roll with his boyz and is now serving a life sentence for murder. Such a senseless waste of lives.

The girls

The girls were kept separate. They were a sad bunch of fighters who were very difficult to manage. I found a few magic words that were almost a guarantee to win them over or to at least get them to talk. If I were to simply sit down next to someone and softly say, "You look like you are about ready to explode" or "Do you feel like you are drowning?" This almost always opened up the lines of communication. They felt I understood them. Tears would flow. A sad white girl by the name of Tina was always leaving for court and always returning. Nothing was ever settled with her due to family members failing to show up, time after time. Finally, she was heading to court right before Christmas. The teaching staff wished her well, as we were leaving for our well deserved Christmas vacation.

Two weeks later, after the first of the year, we returned. There she was. She had spent the entire vacation behind bars. She told me that her dad had a cold and was unable, yet again, to come to court on that day. She needed to be released to family members and no one was ever there for her. I know there are always two or more sides to every story, however, once again, if I were her mother, I don't think she would have found herself in that situation. I don't think a cold would have kept me from a court appearance on behalf of my daughter.

Playing games with these kids took lots of organizational skills. The game we played was Scattergories! I highly recommend this game. First of all, these kids, for the most part, are not used to adults wanting to play games with them. They love it! Even those who refused in the beginning, found they could not help but join in once they understood it is not difficult and it makes fools of no one. It is best to attempt this game after an understanding of the players is acquired, because they must be broken down into workable teams. There is one die to be rolled. This die has many sides all containing letters of the alphabet. The teams have lists of all different categories. The timer is started and the players must respond to all the categories with words that start with the letter that was rolled. Someone on each team is the designated writer. I strategically teamed up readers with non-readers, members of opposing gangs, and experienced players with non-experienced players. I would soon observe them whispering to each other, strategizing, giving high fives, laughing, and jumping out of their seats. This game is what I would bribe them with in order to get work out of them. They craved it. They couldn't wait for the next round. Guards would come to my door due to the noise. It was joyful noise. It was something to behold. Guards even asked to participate, which made it even more fun.

Sean

The "box" at the end of the hallway was for punishment and isolation. No one wanted to go to the "box". If a teacher summoned a correction officer to his or her classroom with a removal request, that was where he or she was headed, to the "box". Also, we each had what was known as a "panic button" on our wall by the door. In five years I pushed the "panic button" once. Sean was escorted out and I never had to see him again. He scared me. He and his friend were in for the horrific torture and murder of a social worker whom they had abducted from a local mall during the

Christmas shopping season. The facts of exactly how she died were a mystery. The exit wound was through her shoulder, but there was no trace of an entry wound. What this animal shared with another inmate, who ultimately shared with me, was that he had inserted the gun into her vagina and shot the damn thing. Within the walls of my small classroom, he roamed like a caged animal. He would not sit down and tried to intimidate me with his stares. He went to the "box" and was ultimately shipped to the justice center where he was housed and tried as an adult. Because I used my "panic button" only once, the word spread of what had happened to me. The guards and the principal checked to make sure I was O.K. The word also got back to me when Sean supposedly killed himself while incarcerated downtown. The inside word was that although it was made to look like a suicide, it was a case of street justice taking its course. It hurts me to refer to anyone as an animal. One thing is for sure, and that is that that young man did not grow up under ideal circumstances. He was a white boy who grew up in a family of Hell's Angels. He probably grew up fighting for survival all his life. Once again, I found myself thinking that if he'd had me for a mom, he would not have been in that situation. Poor thing, but his problems are now over. Years later, as a follow-up to this story, his mother's dismembered body was found in the trunk of a car.

Faulty parenting

I found that many of our repeat white population were the wildflowers of our local Hell's Angels. One such boy took my heart. Johnny was his name and he was one whom I was told had literally grown up in the system. He and many of his cousins made it a revolving door, a true challenge to stay out of trouble. He was well known among the teachers as a pretty funny kid. He liked to sit next to me in class. I guess that made him feel special and I liked him. One morning, while in class, I received a personal call that my closest girlfriend had been in a terrible car accident and I was needed at the hospital. When I returned from the phone call, I told the class I'd be leaving for the day and Johnny asked what was wrong. I told him and the only reason I told him was because he asked. I found that a white woman with a job, a home and a car doesn't get much sympathy from these wildflowers. No matter what the case, their stories match or beat hers. It was always best to keep any personal drama to myself. He said he hoped everything worked out for her and for me. When I returned in a couple of days, he'd been shipped out to serve his sentence.

Over a year later, here came Johnny into my classroom once again. He took his seat next to me, just like before. He leaned into me and inquired about my girlfriend, who had since passed away. He said he was so very sorry. I was so amazed that he'd even remembered my problem and I told him so. With his sorted, dangerous, thug lifestyle, who would think that he had room in his memory bank for anyone else's problems. He leaned into me and simply said, "That's just the kinda guy I am." I wonder where he is today. I wonder if he escaped his prison legacy. I think he had a heart of gold, and not much guidance.

Another poor soul that took my heart with him was a black boy named Adonis. He was a murderer. Adonis used to cut other teachers' classes to spend more time with me because he liked the stories I read to them. Many of the incarcerated kids could not read, because they had spent too much time running the streets instead of going to school. I would read stories I thought would be valuable to them. Adonis loved it and me. Those teachers whose classes he cut, just let him come to me. He became known as my "teacher's pet". The day of his trial and sentencing arrived and I asked that the security escorts please bring him back afterwards so that I could say good bye to him. He'd been there with us for almost a year. They accommodated me and brought him back. His sentence was forty-four years and we hugged good-bye at my door. Adonis's story is a very sad one. He was a product of our less than perfect foster system. From his social workers I learned that he was removed from his mother's care when he was three because, among other things, her method of punishment was to burn him on his legs with the bottoms of her hot pots and pans. She attended his sentencing. He was moved from foster home to foster home, never quite adjusting to the world around him. It was told to me that when the incident happened he was living at the local Y.M.C.A. He shot and killed an innocent man who was using a pay phone. The boys who were with him gave the account that Adonis wanted to know what it was like to kill someone. The story goes that the man he killed had just become engaged the night before and was on the phone with his fiancé at the time of his death. Don't get me wrong, Adonis is indeed where he belongs, however, there are reasons for behaviors in this world, not excuses, reasons.

The reason I functioned so well within the walls of the slammer, is because I believed that most of the inmates were there as a result of faulty parenting. The rate at which fourteen year old children are becoming mothers is staggering. What real chance at survival and success does a child have whose mother gave birth at fourteen? Dr. Phil explains this so well. He has said, on more than a few occasions, that the opposite sex parent is crucial to the formation of the character, self-esteem, and soul of a child. Let's face it, the number of intact homes with both biological parents under the same roof is small. Many of the fathers of my students were absent in some way. They were either incarcerated, dead, or unknown. Dr. Phil goes on to explain the obvious. If a little girl is raised with her dad telling her every day that she is beautiful, brilliant, wonderful, worthy, unique, valuable, and perfect, this little girl is most likely not at risk of falling behind a bush or into the back seat of a car with the first guy that says something nice to her. She'll be used to it. She'll already know it. She'll grow up feeling that the guy, whomever he may be, is the lucky one to be with her.

When I would present this idea to a class, which I often did, the reactions were much like that of a light bulb going off. Girls and women are emotional beings. We love to love and be loved. We respond to kindness. We fall in love with and misinterpret the act of sex; especially young girls. The little kids raised in the ghetto or the projects have very slim perimeters. They know their neighbors and don't usually expand their horizons. They are insulated and stay close to home. They go from playing with the kids in the hood, to having sex with the kids in the hood. Many have babies with the boyz in the hood. I've known boys who have fathered babies with multiple girls in my classes. These boys honor no one. The girls couldn't care less. Now they, and their young mothers, who are now grandmothers at thirty, have someone to love!

Most parents, even young ones, love their offspring, but if you don't know how to parent, there could very well be disastrous results. An explanation is needed here, just to clarify that not every move a child makes can be blamed on the parents. Just like parents cannot assume credit for all the good our kids do and accomplish, it's only realistic to know that decisions are made that are completely independent of one's home training. After all, there are preachers' children who take a wrong turn. For the most part, I viewed my inmate wildflowers as having gotten a raw deal in the parent department.

Just like any other school environment, we had students with handicaps. They had everything from bullet wounds that didn't kill them, to a child with six fingers, deaf kids, and a guy with one eye. The guy with one eye was a victim of a shooting when he was a very young child. He was just in the wrong place at the wrong time and caught a stray bullet. He was a very sweet young man whose crime I never was privy to. He liked me and liked sitting next to me in front of the class. This was a class of the older boys. The doors of our classrooms were revolving doors, to say the least. Every day, every class period, we could expect new arrivals. A new arrival entered and took a back seat. He was a cocky young man with lots of facial hair. He commenced to flirting with me, the teacher. My usual response to such nonsense was to say that I did not sweat the small stuff and to laugh it off. My one-eyed friend took offence to this guy's advances toward his teacher. When he had had enough, he stood up, pointed to my face and said, "Hey man, if ya look real close . . . . SHE OLD!" He thought that would stop the nonsense once and for all. It's become a line my family uses time and again when referring to my age.

You are out

After five very rewarding years of teaching in this very special school, I was forced out. A new principal came on board, a white man around my own age. The rumor was that he was having marital problems and was a drinker. I was so very comfortable and well respected by, not only the staff, but by the kids as well. I remember one time in particular when I was summoned to court out of a class. The principal said he would sit in for me, thinking it would certainly not be too long. Well, he was wrong. I was gone quite a long while and when I arrived he literally ran from my room. Sometimes administrators forget what it's like to be a teacher. The boys had given him a very hard time and wanting to save face, he did not call for back up, because I never called for backup. Maybe this was the beginning of the end for me.

Toward the end of the year, this genius formulated new guidelines for his staff of ten teachers. He decided that he wanted everyone to have double or triple certification. Knowing that we only offered the basics to these incarcerated teens, dual certification never really mattered. I was his target because I was certified only in English, and so far, that had served me well. On his spread sheet, it was clear that I was the teacher that did not qualify and had to be eliminated. I could not believe it. If something is not broken, why try to fix it? Right? Wrong. I worried all summer, hoping things would go my way. I even swallowed my pride and placed a couple of heartfelt phone calls to this man's home during the summer, to which he lied and said that he would do all he could on my behalf. All along, he had an agenda. When school opened in the fall and I was placed elsewhere, I soon was informed that this jerk had appointed his mousey little girlfriend into my slot, my classroom. He had been kicked out of his marital home, away from his wife and three sons, and was now living with this English teacher. In order to keep an eye on her, he hired her. Some of the faculty kept me abreast of the dealings within the detention center. I was told that the mousey girlfriend was not well suited for the job at all and would lay on her panic button all day, every day. She became very close to having a nervous breakdown. He was often found leaving the teachers' lounge smelling strongly of liquor. It was awful.

Then, one evening I got the call. This principal had killed himself. He did the carbon monoxide thing in his garage . . . . and he took his kids' dog with him! This is the man that changed the course of my professional life. This is the man who made decisions, all on his own, so he could keep an eye on his girlfriend. She hated it there; I was missed there. The morale of the school was damaged. More attention should have been paid to this man and his drinking problem.

Chapter 8

Back on the outside

It is human nature to resist change. Whenever I had to relocate, whether it was due to a lay-off or some other shuffling of faculty, I hated it. I always felt I would never adjust, never be happy, but I was wrong every single time. The school to which I was relocated following my removal from the slammer was a gift. Special, lovable kids are everywhere. I was welcomed with open arms into this faculty and was very, very happy for another five years, until it closed and everyone was once again, spread out all over the city.

Mitchell

Mitchell comes to my mind. He was a special education student whom I came to know because his teacher's classroom was across the hall from mine. I covered his teacher's classes every now and then for various reasons and, as a result, got to know her students. Mitchell was one of those students who loved to be helpful. He'd offer to wash the blackboards, sweep the floors, or straighten the desks. We became friends, mostly because I had no real authority over him. I learned from Mitchell that he was being raised by his wheelchair-bound grandmother, because his mom was in prison. This grandmother was raising about seven of her grandchildren due to similar circumstances.

When a grandparent becomes a parent it's sometimes not a happy situation. When it becomes an overwhelming burden, this is when the sweet grandmother image ceases to be. This family of children were almost all labeled "special" and were all running wild.

They followed no rules because there were no consequences . . . . because the grandmother was in a wheelchair!

I found Mitchell to be very sweet, charming, funny, and helpful. Once I asked him if his grandmother thought he was funny. He said, "I don't be funny in front of her. She just thinks I be bad." Mitchell knew I had his back. He'd run the halls like he ran the streets. He'd play "cat and mouse" with the security staff. Within the confines of our walls, he knew he was safe. He was a small kid, so he was regarded as cute. He'd knock on my door and ask if I would hide him, "Cuz they be after me!" I always played along and whatever class I had in front of me loved that I would. He would play it up big and hide under my desk. When Security came knocking, they knew damn well he was with me, but in the hood "snitches get stitches", so they'd let it go with a wink, knowing that Mitchell was at least safe.

Special incentive programs were always being implemented when we received federal or state money. One such program was for the purpose of after school tutoring. The teachers were paid per student per hour. The students also earned $100 if they attended on time every single day after school. We followed a curriculum expressly designed for each enrollee. After months of participating, I ended up with just two students who were dedicated enough to stay every day after school with me. Mitchell was one of those two. The other was a young lady, Gina, who was bright and focused. She was in it for the money. Mitchell sat with me at my desk and we worked so well together, while Gina preferred to be on her own. One day, toward the end of the program, I asked Mitchell what he planned to do with his money. He thought for quite a while, looked at Gina and me and said, "I need sox".

Of course I bought Mitchell plenty of sox, so he wouldn't have to spend his money on them, for which he was grateful. I believe he bought some electronics with his hard earned money.

Everyone knew Mitchell was one of my special guys. If his teacher, or a substitute for his teacher, was having a hard time with him, they knew they could send him to me. No matter what I was doing, my door was open to Mitchell. He would act out on purpose because he wanted to be sent to me!

One day our principal came to me with some bad news. My little bad Mitchell at age fifteen, for all intents and purposes, had had a heart-related attack and was in the I.C.U. in a children's hospital. The principal arranged to have my classes covered, so I could leave school immediately to go see him. He was in isolation and only family members were to be admitted. Now Mitchell is black and I am white, but it seemed to make no difference to the nurses because he had received no visitors at all. As a matter of fact, the entire time he was in the hospital the only visitors he'd received were teachers. The nurse opened the big glass doors and led me to his bed. He was hooked up to everything under the sun and looked awful to me. We sat and held hands. We didn't need to talk. He did, however, tell me he liked it there and that he liked the food, and that the nurses were real cool. There was a long list of things Mitchell was going to have to change when he was released from the hospital in order to stay healthy.

That weekend I attended a local "Healing" service with which my sister is involved. I took a picture of Mitchell with me. We prayed so hard for this little man's recovery. That Monday I was in front of a morning class when the principal sent someone to summon me to her office. I arrived, not knowing what to expect. She said, "We have a surprise for you, Ms. Fitch." Out from around the corner, after being out for only one week, came Mitchell. He was as happy to see me as I was to see him. I often wonder how much of an influence on his recovery was my trip to the 'Healing' service. And then I realized that Mitchell never had medical insurance. Maybe that had something to do with his speedy release.

 ## Clyde

Another young man who was being raised by his grandmother was Clyde. Clyde was enrolled in our special after hours program called "The Twilight Program". The school spent the entire first semester identifying those students who had the power to ruin and disrupt our days. These were the chronic fighters, chronic class cutters, chronic late arrivals, chronic hall-walkers, and those re-entering following incarceration. When the names were compiled, the second semester commenced with our "Twilight Program" which was held from 2:30, after the regular school was dismissed, until 6:30. We had our administrators, our security guards, our lunches, and our late buses to deliver them home. Clyde was one of these students.

Due to the disruptive nature of these dysfunctional wildflowers and the special skills and temperament required to deal with them, few teachers opted for these positions. The first year of "Twilight" there was a huge perk that no one really expected: a four-day work week with Fridays off! I just figured realistically that no administrators, security guards, or bus drivers wanted to work until after dark, in this neighborhood, especially on Fridays.

We worked well for a few weeks, until the rest of the faculty got wind of our four-day work week. They complained that they too had rough times, and that it was simply not fair. Even when reminded that anyone could have applied, they still balked . . . . and won. We ultimately had to tell our students that they now had to start attending on Fridays. I was shocked as to how many actually attended! They were all the boys. They were all motherless boys, who came to school to see us. They also came for lunch, and never missed a day. Clyde was hard core. He even had the facial hair of a full grown man. He'd been incarcerated. To many, he was scary, until you got to know him. Clyde lived with his grandmother, who was raising all of her many grandchildren because all of her biological children, including Clyde's mother, were in prison. One might first think, what a wonderful, giving woman. Then, one might wonder, where did she go wrong, that all of her offspring ended up imprisoned? Anyway, she ran a day care center. Not only did she care for her own grandchildren, she also was paid to take in more. Clyde had duties every morning and night with these charges, one of whom was his own daughter. No wonder he came to school every day. It was better than babysitting!

I continued my habit of hugging the students on their way in and out of my classroom even in this "Twilight" setting. They too took this seriously and it always set the stage for our days. Clyde, like I said, was one who was conscientious about his attendance and his hugs. One day, at the beginning of the month, he came in and announced to me that he was just stopping in to say hi and to get his hug, but that he couldn't stay. When I asked what was up, he responded, that, "The block is hot." The significance of it being the first of the month was that government checks were issued at that time and cash was plentiful, especially on the block!

I also came to be aware that attendance was down throughout the system at the beginnings of each month. People were food and clothing shopping. By the end of the month, however, attendance was up again because the cupboards were now bare and school served both breakfast and lunch.

One could be pretty sure of the foods that were being purchased in these homes. Obesity was and continues to be, rampant due to fast foods and junk foods. The smell of Doritos was common in our classrooms, whether it be morning or "Twilight" school, and Cokes were always the drink of choice. McDonald's is referred to as a restaurant, and babies are raised on this food from the time they cut their first teeth.

I have known more than a few teenagers who were sadly not the least bit embarrassed by the fact that they could not squeeze into the desks. These obese kids had to sit in chairs at tables that were not attached. I saw girls at our dances and at our proms who were sporting dresses that revealed their midriffs, which was a huge spare tire around their middle. It often crossed my mind that although their self esteem was enviable, it seemed no mirrors were available for these young ladies. Who, I wondered, were these girls' role models? What was to become of them if these were their bodies as teenagers?

Duran

Speaking of government checks, there was a very well dressed young man by the name of Duran, who happened to be a special education student. He was in my class due to the mainstreaming of special education students. He seemed to be doing just fine. I met his mother who seemed so very proud when I mentioned how well dressed she kept her son. Soon after meeting her, Duran stopped in, wearing yet another new outfit. I was totally curious as to how this single mom could afford these marvelous outfits because I knew there were other siblings. Duran was very forthcoming with this very confidential information. He said, "My mama gets 'crazy checks' for all of us. I could have her show you how you could get 'crazy checks' too." The scam this woman was cleverly pulling off was to program her kids to respond correctly when being tested for special education purposes. I was aware, and now understood, why Duran didn't seem any different from the average kid. All four of this woman's kids were labeled as special education students and received monthly government checks as a result. I never knew what his mother said to him for revealing this private scam to me, however, I never saw her again.

Within my home nail business I have a client with two severely handicapped adult sons. They are both non-verbal, diaper-wearing adult men who must be bathed and shaved every day. This lady has had to dig and scratch for every nickel she's ever received from the government. What she really needs is a crash course from Duran's mother on how to get those damn "crazy checks"!

Chapter 9

The Story of Emanuel

This is the story of Emanuel. If I had to name a favorite student over my thirty year career, it would be Emanuel. He made a huge impact on my life. He was different. You may remember my mention of him when I wrote earlier about my practice of hugging the students on the way in and on the way out of my classes. He was the boy who said, "I don't hug." The one with whom I've remained friends and in contact with as an adult. The one who asked me to marry him . . . . that was Emanuel. He was a gifted writer and a rapper. He schooled me and turned me on to the art of rap music and the understanding of the lyrics. We would compare and analyze the differences and similarities between rap music and country music. He taught me that both tell life stories. Both are very heartfelt and sad. Hearts break no matter who you are or what kind of music you prefer.

Emanuel was an old soul. He never felt that he fit in. He always removed himself from the masses. He even chose, right from the start, to seat himself at my desk, instead of out in the classroom. It was always O.K. with me because, like I said, the classroom was my stage and I was the star, and the star never sat. Emanuel was an observer and a listener. He never participated in the drama of the classes or the drama of the halls. He was attracted to the quiet girls. We bonded initially during our many fire drills. Our city's schools were hated by the fire departments, because it was the law that they had to respond to all alarms. The kids pulled the alarms so the entire school population would empty into the parking lot, while the firemen searched the school and sounded an all-clear bell. We sometimes had up to six drills in a day and it never mattered what the weather was doing. The motivation was, most of the time, for fighting. When everyone would pile back into the building, so would some "outsiders". The fights would commence and more alarms would sound. I remember a fireman yelling out of the truck, "Who's running this nut house?"

Anyway, while the craziness was going on, Emanuel and I would be wandering out in the field, talking, waiting for the all-clear bell. A connection was forever made. It was arranged, by us, that I was his English teacher for tenth, eleventh, and twelfth grades. His papers were read to the classes as shining examples of how it was done. I looked forward to his opinions, points of view, and comments. I've saved them. When it came time for our annual award ceremony, it was like Michael Jackson at the Grammys. He was told to just wait on the stage, because there were so many awards, mostly from me: best student, best writer, and most likely to succeed.

I was involved with the senior prom the year he graduated. What an event! The girls began searching in September, for the perfect color, the perfect dress, and finding the perfect date. I swear the dressmaker for the local strippers had more business than she could handle.

As I mentioned, I have a small, enjoyable business/hobby on the side as a nail tech. I work out of my house and during prom time, my business boomed . . . pro-bono, of course. Emanuel and his then girlfriend came home with me after school, days before the prom, to tend to Anastasia's nails. Emanuel sat in the T.V. room with my dog, being as patient as ever. I drove them home and Ana was dropped off first, because she had an appointment with her dressmaker. Emanuel and I sat in his driveway promising each other we would stay in contact after graduation. His nosey little sister came running out to the car wanting to know who this white lady was in her driveway with her big brother.

Our high schools have what is known as the "Line Up" right before the prom, where they arrive at their school's parking lot in what could very well be compared to a "Red Carpet" event. Neighbors bring their lawn chairs, teachers bring their cameras, and I brought my daughter-in-law. The graduates slowly bump their way through the parking lot in their tricked out rides. Emanuel's father, not only rented a limo for the occasion, he also rented a tuxedo for himself as the driver to ensure his son's and his date's safety. I was so impressed. All the kids looked like a million bucks. Students attended even if they were pregnant, if they had a date or not, and everyone enjoyed his and her fifteen minutes of fame. I danced with my sweet young man at the prom. Everyone knew we would.

At graduation is where I finally met his mom, who was dealing with fighting some form of cancer. She was very quiet and reserved. His dad, however, wanted to make sure I would not lose track of our boy. We talked on the phone here and there, always exchanging, 'I love you'. He enrolled in college and lives rolled on. A couple years later I tried to find him on Facebook, but I knew better. He was not the type. I did, however, put my feelers out, and eventually I found him. His former prom date provided me with his number and informed him that I was looking for him. I called and we got together. He was still living with his mom and had no cell phone. He didn't want one. He thought it would be a bother and he wanted to be in charge of who he talked to and when. He regarded cell phones as weapons used to keep track of people and he didn't want to be kept track of or stalked.

We went out to lunch and he insisted on paying. He was working as a welder and was preparing to graduate from a welding school. He shared with me how he was saving his money by living at home and caring for his mother. He told me of the girlfriends he had lost, their complaint being that he was too boring. He said he continues to feel that he doesn't fit in. Emanuel always listened to my advice concerning birth control. I always told my classes to control it themselves and to believe no one. He insisted he never wanted kids because he didn't want to bring them into this world.

After lunch we headed downtown, so he could demonstrate to me how guys shop for the perfect outfit. I'll bet you didn't know that it all starts with the hat! He bought an entire outfit, including the shoes, and insisted on buying me a purse for my birthday. We'd had a wonderful day walking around downtown, holding hands like the best of friends that we were. We always believed we were mental soul mates.

A few months rolled by and on Friday, March 1, 2013, I received a text from Emanuel. He'd finally gotten a cell phone! His text said he wanted a date. The next night was a Saturday, date night.

I texted for him to be there at eight. He arrived at four! We went to a neighborhood restaurant where we were able to talk and talk. He told me he was now employed at a small welding factory where he was, not only the youngest, but the only black employee among older, white guys, whom he felt were "picking on him". He wanted my advice. The example he gave me was of some wise cracks regarding his fashionable sagging pants. He said that so far he was doing the Martin Luther King-thing by not responding at all. He didn't want to engage in what could result in a confrontation. I told him I would give it some thought and get him some sound advice.

We decided we would get together more regularly, since he now had the convenience of his cell phone. He invited me to his dad's church. His father and step mother are co-ministers of their own small Baptist church. We finished our dinners and headed back to my house. When he left, I walked him out to his car where he leaned over to kiss me on my forehead and said, "I've had a date with and kissed Ms. Fitch good night. Now I can die happy!" I smacked his arm and sent him on his way. When I went back in I realized he'd left on the kitchen table his precious hat, the one we bought together. His answer to my text was that he left it on purpose, to keep it because he was coming back.

Two nights later, while I was doing the nails of a client who happens to be an attorney, I ran Emanuel's work story by her and asked what she would advise. She thought about it for a minute and said to tell him that in the working world sometimes we must compromise. She would advise Emanuel to simply pull his pants up while at work and see what a difference it would make for him in the long run. I texted him the next morning that I had some advice that he might not like, but that it was from a worthy source, and that he should call me when he got a chance.

He never got the chance to call me back because that night he'd been shot and killed in the parking lot of a bar he'd stopped at with his brother and his cousin. The calls came to me as the news got out, but I just knew they were mistaken. It just couldn't be my sweet, peaceful Emanuel. But it was. He was gone. May he rest in peace. I will never get over losing Emanuel. The world will never be the same. I believe, as many did, that he was just too good for this world . . . the world in which he said he never felt he fit in.

They say it was a fight. How could it have been a fight? Emanuel was not a fighter. He never participated. He was a big boy at over six foot tall and well over two hundred pounds. I spoke with the police of the city in which it happened. I needed to tell the detective that this was not the murder of a loser, gang-banging, drug running bad boy for whom it was just a matter of time before the inevitable happened. He had to know this was different. He had to know that Emanuel came from a long line of preachers. He attended church regularly where he was also a member of youth groups. This detective was one in a million. He listened to me for over fifteen minutes of his busy day. He wrote down these important facts. He offered me his phone number so that I could easily get in contact with him should I want any updates.

The next three days were an avalanche of sadness and grief. They were days of viewing, church, and the funeral with his entire family and extended church family. Not many former schoolmates were in attendance due to the fact that he was not close to many. These events were filled with loved ones whose hearts were absolutely broken. Saturday was the family viewing, which I received an invitation to attend from his little sister. People were out in the parking lot of the funeral home when I drove in. I stood by my car trying to pull myself together, when his younger half-brother approached me saying, "I know who you are. He loved you". I looked up to see his father approaching me, walking just like his son and looking just like him. We hugged and he took my hand and led me inside. People were falling apart. It became real. His mother looked like a zombie. His male friends and cousins were crying out loud. His father appeared to be trying to care for those who needed support, after all he is a minister and believes Emanuel is in a better place. It was a sunny day and many were milling around the parking lot after viewing. I wandered over to his dad as he and another preacher were praying. He wanted me to know that there was nothing Emanuel didn't share with him, and he shared with me that Emanuel wanted to marry me. I already knew this and confirmed for his dad that the feelings were mutual. Emanuel always laughed and said, "There is a forty year difference in our ages and after my next birthday, there'll only be thirty-nine!" I told his dad that last Saturday we had made plans for me to attend his church.

His step-mother took my hand and said the invitation stands. She gave me directions and the next morning I attended the sweetest, smallest, little Baptist church service where everyone was singing, dancing, praising, and mourning Emanuel. He introduced me as the teacher that Emanuel wanted to marry. It was gut-wrenching, but I felt there was a reason for me to be there. I'll most probably return. I was among people who all loved Emanuel.

The funeral was the next day, Monday. My wonderful son, who never had the pleasure of meeting Emanuel, but had heard much about him, arranged to be with me for the whole day's events. This took place in a huge family church where there was standing room only. The stream of visitors was constant. As we passed by his casket, people were falling apart and helping each other all over this enormous room. The music was constant. His parents and family had front row seats where they greeted all who entered to say our final good-byes to Emanuel. On this day his father was a different color. Today was the reality of the death of his only child. All he could offer were hugs. It was pitiful. There were preachers from ten surrounding Baptist churches all having personally known Emanuel and had stories of his childhood within their churches. They all spoke and sang of him lovingly. The oldest preacher even broke into a rap in honor of our boy. Even my son was shedding tears. This funeral lasted for over two hours, but it seemed like much less. He deserved every minute of the celebration of his wonderful life. It was said that everyone makes choices every day, all day, and the choice he made to go to that bar put him in the wrong place at the wrong time. It was said that if he'd made a different choice, he'd most certainly be with us today, but the Lord called him and he went.

By now it was raining and the cars were lining up to proceed to the cemetery. We decided to leave because of babysitters and jobs awaiting. I'd seen and felt enough. When I arrived home I placed a call to the police station. I left a message as to who I was and within a ten minute period, the detective returned my call. Again, I was so impressed that he even cared. He asked about the family and the events of the past couple of days. He informed me that they had two of the men responsible and a warrant out for the third. As I believed right from the beginning, it was not about Emanuel. A fight broke out and he was trying to pull his friend out of the mess, when someone got a gun and used it to kill Emanuel. My son said, after witnessing the unbelievable grief, that these monsters, who so easily snuffed out the life of their fellow human being, should be made to witness the inconsolable suffering they have caused for so very many families. We wonder if it would make a difference, however, the damage was already done.

I was so very impressed with the concern the detective had shown that I decided to take it a little further and called his superior. Through my tears, I told the chief of police who I was and what I'd been doing all day and that his detective had gone above and beyond for a young man they had collected from a local bar parking lot in their district the previous Tuesday. He too was wonderful to me. He too inquired as to the family and how they were doing. He said he rarely receives such calls on behalf of his detectives and truly appreciated it. He also offered his phone number in the event that I would want any more updates. All of these wonderful, concerned people were there because of who Emanuel was. He will live on in my heart forever.

Within two months of her wonderful son's untimely death, Emanuel's mother died. She had been continuing to battle her cancer, but my belief is that she simply gave up and died of a broken heart.

Chapter 10

Rodney

I have weathered more than my share of funerals for young black males. None were easy. All were cut down way too early. Every family suffered. Rodney was shot and killed two years before Emanuel. At our last dinner, Emanuel and I even spoke of him, because they were in the same class. Emanuel said that he had to be honest in his assessment of Rodney as, "Looking for trouble. He was always flashing his money around, just asking for trouble", is what Emanuel said of him. Rodney was a less than confident young man. He was a good looking, light-skinned boy whose mother was white and his father was black. He was not the brightest of students, however, he put forth a lot of effort and thrived on praise, as most of us do. He was also in my English class for most of high school.

There is a term in my professional world known as C.P.T. Those of us in the know, are aware of the meaning as 'Colored People Time'. The meaning behind this is that, as a rule, at least in the hood, they are late! I never quite understood where the passive aggressive act originated, other than the control. I even had a black female principal remark to me about a chronically late young white teacher that she was somehow on C.P.T.! This teacher was late every day due to having to drop off her two children and then make her daily stop at Starbucks for God's sake! Think how this blatant behavior must have made her waiting students feel. When steps were taken, after several warnings, to curtail this disrespectful and unacceptable behavior, she was told she would now be docked every time. She had the nerve to respond to this disciplinary action by claiming discrimination!

She was not alone, strolling in late. Many, many were chronically late. As a result, students were late and school-wide attendance was held back until our second block, giving everybody ample time to arrive and be counted as present. It was all about the numbers that were sent down town. I always arrived on time, with time to spare for preparations and to provide my classroom as a safe place for those few students who were roaming the halls awaiting their teachers' late arrivals. It was a meeting place. Having a first period class on my schedule was wonderful, mostly because the class time was cut in half. I swear the kids came to school when they woke up. They didn't wake up to come to school!

My eyes were opened as to the magnitude of this problem one year when I opted to teach summer school. As I prepared for my classes, I assumed that I would be saddled with a bunch of dummies who failed their English classes that year. This was not the case at all. The fact of the matter was that it was a room full of bright students who happened to have their English classes scheduled for first period the previous year! They simply didn't get up and go to school. They had planned all along on making it up in summer school. It was O.K. with them. Their safe, social life at school will continue throughout the summer. Their free breakfasts and lunches will continue to be provided, and it is a well known fact that summer school is a condensed version of what is presented during the school year. It is easier, more laid back, and we had a great time . . . all because of C.P.T.

Some had to ride more than one bus, some walked and some got rides. Rodney was one who was there on time, every day because he got a ride from his working mom or dad. He shared with me how afraid he was of the streets. He was not a big boy, nor was he an accomplished fighter. The main reason he woke up in time to be driven was that he did not want to be walking the streets on his way to school. He was so afraid. He chilled with me every morning. We had breakfast together. Once our pattern was established, I made sure to bring breakfast for two. We worked together on Rodney's senior papers, assigned by me. We talked about girls. We talked about sports. We talked about family. He was so proud to have had private tutoring, which produced perfect papers, that he readily shared with his classmates. I used his papers as examples whenever I could, just to see his beaming face. He'd run errands for me during class time because his work was already completed. I loved me some Rodney!

Rodney had a job. He worked at night, cleaning a building down town, with his mother. Like I said, Rodney was not the brightest of students. He was a bit of a show-off, when it came to the money he was making. I warned him about flashing his "Benjamins". He was so eager to impress both girls and guys with his money, he would bring them out all too often.

Now, when spring arrived and it was time for the prom, Rodney had no date. This, however, did not stop him. He showed up to our "Line Up", dressed in a beautiful white tux, with lime green accessories, right down to his lime green alligator shoes. I took many wonderful pictures of my proud graduate.

The news came to me the following March. Rodney had been shot and killed, five houses from his own. He was found underneath a car. The story was that it was a pay day for Rodney. A "friend" had set him up to meet at a certain place and time. Wanting to fit in and be a big deal with his cash, Rodney was unsuspecting. His mother says that they chased him, shot him, and stuffed him underneath the car. I, however, believe differently. I believe that he was being chased and hid under the car, where they found and shot him. They were never, to my knowledge, caught and brought to justice.

Rodney's funeral was another grueling event. It was just a year following graduation and was filled with many of those who graduated with Rodney. I was compelled to speak. I had written a short speech, telling everyone how we had bonded over breakfast for the past two years, and how much I would miss him. The funeral had been delayed quite a long while due to the family's lack of funds. Finally, due to various donations, the family was able to bury their only son. I visited his mother soon after, to share some of Rodney' papers I'd saved. I also learned that the family had no pictures, other than those taken from phones. I, however, had all those wonderful shots of him, styling and profiling at the prom. I promised to return. I had prints made of various sizes, matted, and framed them all. When I returned I could feel how grateful they were for all of them. I was so happy I could do something, anything. The family has since moved away from the location that will forever be the spot where Rodney died. I think of them often and wonder how they are surviving without their wonderful Rodney.

At one point, during a rash of funerals for the young black men in my personal world, I'd decided to attend no more. I left each one feeling so enraged by the undignified behaviors displayed by those who attended. I witnessed, on more than a few occasions, people attempting to climb into the casket. I witnessed fights breaking out between girls who were under the false impression they were the only girlfriend of the deceased. There were girls alleging to be a girlfriend just to claim the attention of her loss. It always made me so mad and I always preached the next day in school as to the appropriate etiquette expected at a funeral. I'd explain that while these attention whores are doing what they're doing, the attention is taken away from the unfortunate victim in the casket. Man power must now be directed to the fight or to the person casket diving. Quiet, dignified, under the radar behavior is expected by all those attending to pay their respects.

Leroy

Leroy was shot, but lived to tell about it. Leroy was a quiet young man who was new to our school and had only a few friends. The girls loved him. He was a well dressed kid, who loved his shoes. Shoes are such a status symbol in the hood. New ones were worn with the price tags sometimes proudly displayed for all to see. New hats were worn also with tags revealing their value. The word came in that he had been shot and that he was in the ICU in a nearby hospital. After school I made my way to this hospital to see for myself his condition. He was alone, unconscious, and hooked up to so many horrifying tubes that all I could do was stand there and stare. He was swollen and unrecognizable. As I looked around the room, I focused on the shelves on the other side of his bed. Among other personal possessions were his shoes, his new shoes that he was so very proud of just the day before, only now they had blood on them. We kept track of his condition and recovery, but Leroy never returned to our school. He was in a rehab center for quite a while, and I supposed his mother felt the need to move away, far away.

Chapter 11

Personal Hygiene

Every year, teachers are presented with a new crop of other people's kids. As hard as we may try to show no favoritism, it is human nature to be drawn to some more than others. There are always those kids with personal hygiene problems. Phillip was the stinky tenth grader this particular year. He had a strong odor that was a combination of urine, body odor, and dirty tennis shoes. It was awful and he became, of course, a target. Surprisingly, the others tried to be nice, however, Phillip never took their gentle hints.

Usually a hygiene issue would be turned over to a health or physical education teacher, but the kids came to me, asking for my intervention. They said, "You have to do something." I asked Phillip to see me after school. Ever so gingerly, I told him he needed to attend to personal cleanliness more now that he is a teenager. Complimenting teens usually does the trick. I told him that because he was so handsome, he should be expecting attention from girls and he would definitely want to be looking good and smelling good when it happens. He told me that he slept in a bed that he shared with little brothers. I surmised that these were diaper wearing brothers that soaked through their diapers, and sheet laundering was not high priority in Phillip's house.

He returned to school the next day smelling good, or at least, not smelling. The class responded with kindness and compliments, however, it soon returned to the way it was. My next tactic was to call his mother to schedule a meeting. Imagine my surprise when a nurse walked into my classroom and introduced herself as Phillip's mother! How could this be? She spoke of how Phillip didn't like to take showers and how she was "always on him" about it. She took no responsibility and nothing came of this encounter either. Poor Phillip.

This was not the only time I was asked to intervene with a stinky kid. I had a huge revelation late one night and the next day I poured my soul out with a stellar performance to a class with a speech I entitled, "Dead Stuff Stinks", which I kicked around as a possible children's book to be used as a personal hygiene teaching tool. It was a gift!

This was one of those teaching experiences that could never be duplicated. It was from a higher power, and I made a difference that day. I began talking about how dead animals in the yard smell. I spoke of how our garbage and our garbage cans smell. I spoke of how our skin cells are constantly replacing themselves and that's where dust comes from. If food particles are left behind in our teeth, it could very well be meat, dead meat, and dead stuff stinks. Our dead cells need to be washed away. All the dead cells in our bed sheets need to be washed away. I supplied everyone in the class with dental floss and they were educated as to the simplistic reasons for bad breath. It was one of those wonderful days. I loved it and went home dreaming of a book deal. Teachers need to know how to address this delicate issue, because there will always be those kids whose parents don't devote time to personal hygiene instruction.

Chapter 12

Foster Care

Within every school system are the homeless, and those within the foster care system. There are many stories of those who become foster parents for the money they make every month per child. I knew two girls who were living in a foster home down the street from our school. They were among the best dressed kids in the building. They referred to these wonderful foster parents as their parents. Both girls had been removed from their dreadful biological situations. These girls took me home to introduce me to these loving foster parents and to show off their home. I was so very impressed and happy for their good luck at having been placed in such loving circumstance. It was a very clean and well organized home. The back yard was decked out and even had a trampoline. They told me of their annual summer family vacations. The monthly money they received was well and fairly distributed, which explained the girls' wardrobes. The kids all had their own spaces in their bedrooms. Unlike normal foster arrangements, time was not up for them at eighteen years of age. They were off to college, but had a home to return to for as long as they wanted. These people warmed my heart. I have run into these girls since graduation over ten years ago, only to find they remain one huge, loving family. The girls have married. One has children of her own and provides a loving home, which she learned how to do from her foster parents, while the other has married and remained childless. Both have grown into happy, productive members of society.

Monique

All too often the stories are not so happy. Monique was in tenth grade when I met her. She was an extremely obese young girl, who was removed from her home because her mother chose to protect Monique's older brother. This brother was raping Monique and when she reported it, action was taken by removing Monique! She was placed in a foster home that requested newborns and teenagers. Their motivation was for the teens to care for the infants, so they might be off to Las Vegas for their carefree weekends. I wouldn't have believed it if I hadn't witnessed it with my own eyes. Monique and I became very close. She was another one of those "old souls" one runs into throughout one's life. She shared with me that she had never attended a school dance. We had a homecoming dance coming up so I told her we could go together because they were always looking for chaperones. She was all dolled up when I picked her up like a date. We laughed about what losers we both were to be attending the dance with each other, especially her, for attending the dance with an old white woman! She had a great time at this event and I delivered her back home safe and sound.

One of Monique's social workers suggested that she may want to try a weight-loss program. She was very excited about it and decided it was for her. Monique's foster parents were difficult and totally uncooperative throughout. Monique was on her own, but was of course, used to that. I was her cheerleader and promised her that when she reached a certain goal, I would take her out on a shopping spree. She did reach her goal. I picked her up and we went shopping. It was the most wonderful and rewarding experience for me. The clerks got into it with us. We provided for her a true "Pretty Woman" experience. She was dancing in and out of the dressing rooms trying on everything we presented. This was the best and most fun I ever had spending money. We then went out for lunch and I delivered her home with her treasures. The sad news is that very shortly after, Monique gained all her weight back.

Foster Moms

There were quite a few foster mothers on the staff where I taught while I was with Monique. Many of the older women requested newborns, many of which were born addicted to crack. These ladies were seen out in our parking lot trading bassinets, rocking chairs, and other baby amenities. The system paid for day care for those who were working women. Foster care is a very temporary arrangement, especially for newborns who are usually placed relatively soon. It was a revolving door. I was asked, on more than a few occasions, to give it a try, since my son was now in college, and I was experiencing my "empty nest". My reasons were that I could never see myself comfortably returning each baby. I simply was not cut out for it. One such woman, who was down the hall from me, went through a gut-wrenching loss with her foster baby girl. She and her husband, who was an engineer, lived in an affluent part of town and were not doing well with their new "empty nest" situation. They had tried child after child. Some youngsters came to them with their anti-psychotic drugs in tow. They finally were given a newborn baby girl who was born to a crack addicted prostitute and an elderly man. The woman gave birth and immediately signed her over, wanting nothing to do with her. For three years they raised, loved, nurtured, and spoiled their little princess. They enjoyed family vacations and were about to finalize the adoption when Daddy showed up. Daddy was a man near sixty who had no job, no car, and lived in the projects. No one worried. Everyone was sure that common sense would prevail and the girl would remain in the lap of luxury with this loving family. Neither justice nor common sense prevailed. Biological father won his daughter back, and on the designated day, a county van pulled into their driveway, because he had no car, and took her away forever. My fellow teacher and fellow mother took sick and was out for quite a long while. She eventually returned, a little damaged, and vowed to never try the system again.

Chapter 13

Life Lessons

As I said, having changed my major to English has served me well. There is an endless array of topics to discuss and debate and write about, especially when teaching a block schedule where classes were ninety minutes long. I always wondered how a math teacher could keep the class engaged for that length of time. When I had time left over at the end of the block, I would sit on my desk and say, "Let's talk about sex". They loved it. It usually went by way of the sexes complaining about each other and how they are disrespected and cheated on.

I wanted to give these wildflower boys of mine all the worldly advice I gave my own son. I called these "Life lessons". I told them that because they were all so good looking that that made them all good catches. Then, there were those that may have had jobs, of any kind, or those who drove cars. Girls can be very diabolical and sneaky when it comes to getting what they want. For those who want to find a "Baby Daddy", these boys become sitting ducks. I always advised them to trust no one. Be aware that anybody can claim she is taking the pill. Anyone can claim she cannot become pregnant. Anyone can take her pills incorrectly. Anyone can poke a hole in her condom. Boys and men need to take this seriously and take the controlling of births into their own hands.

The story that took everyone aback was about a girl who would tell her current boyfriend she was pregnant, share with him that she was on board with having an abortion if he was willing to pay for it. At the time I was aware of this story, abortions were going for about $250. She would then move on to the next boyfriend/victim and repeat the same scam. She was collecting $250 per boyfriend. Each

93

of these guys were more than willing to come up with this money in order to avoid any babies.

I also liked to preach to them that much like tattoos, babies are permanent. What if one changes his or her mind? Teenagers change their minds all the time, whether it's a favorite color, a favorite song, a favorite outfit, or a mate. The point is that until one is, at the very least, out of his or her teens, a decision to add a new human being to the family should be left alone. I taught my son that men are not ready for permanent relationships, especially babies, until they are in their thirties. Thankfully, he listened to me. My point was that in one's thirties, much of the selfishness may have subsided, and attention can then be devoted to someone else. Lucky babies are those whose parents regard them as gifts from God to be adored and enjoyed, not thought of as a burden or a punishment. I asked the guys to close their eyes and bring to their thoughts the last girlfriend they broke up with and why. Was she a "psycho bitch"? Was she violent? Was she possessive and demanding and selfish and unreasonable? Was she too ghetto? Now, keeping your eyes closed, think about if while you were with her, she had become pregnant. You will have sentenced a perfectly innocent little baby to live with this "psycho bitch" that you couldn't stand for more than a month. They seemed to understand that!

For those young boys who prided themselves on their "Bad Boy" images, I had a message. Being a firm believer in karma, and the idea that what goes around, comes around, I shared my thoughts as to their futures. God will give you baby girls! God will make sure they are beautiful! God will make sure you know that boys like you will be hot on their trails and THAT is what you "Bad Boys" will be living with.

Donte called me from the delivery room. He and Lawanda had been in my English classes all through high school and went to their senior prom together. That was the night they conceived their baby girl! I was right . . . . again! He called to inform me that I had been correct and that she was indeed born beautiful. He would have hell to pay.

Abortions

We would get into spirited debates about abortions. Young people rarely know the exact meaning of "pro-choice". They assume it means pro-abortion. They rarely knew that it meant just what it says . . . freedom to make your own choice about a pregnancy. They were unaware that if one can think of just one scenario where an abortion is warranted, one should be able to obtain one legally. The one instance where we could, most of the time, agree, was over a pregnancy as a result of rape. I had a perfect story to be presented when these debates arose. There was a seventeen year old Hispanic girl in one of my classes in the "slammer". She was the mother of an eight year old boy. She'd been the victim of a gang rape when she was nine years old. Due to the fact that her family was strictly Catholic, abortion was out of the question. They forced her to endure this pregnancy and delivery, and decided to raise this boy as her little brother. This I learned from her social worker, who was located across the hall from my classroom. The girl was not right, as you can well imagine. She was incarcerated for various drug and theft charges. She seemed to me, to be the type who was doomed for a life on the inside. My classes would analyze her situation ad nauseam. They talked about the adoption possibility. They talked about why God allowed this child to be conceived. They talked about how the violent event, pregnancy, and painful birth, would affect a nine year old child. They wondered if the parents cared at all for the emotional welfare of their daughter. At any rate, this was the case I presented every time the abortion issue presented itself.

Large Families

There were the "Life Lesson" talks about the sizes of their future families. Those who proudly announced they desired huge families, with an obscene numbers of children, because they love kids, used to make me crazy. They also believed that growing up with their children was a good thing. To this I would comment that babies deserve for their parents to already be adults. I would respond with questions like, "Do you like doing laundry? Do you like grocery shopping every day? Do you think you'll like planning meals and cooking and cleaning every day for the messes these large numbers of children will create? Do you realize how difficult babies become when they are no longer babies, but spirited teen-agers? Are you aware of the cost of tennis shoes these days?" I tried so very hard to change their inexperienced minds. I educated them as to the perks of having one child, which is what I had as a single mother. I explained to them that he got everything he needed, not having to share with any siblings. When they would comment as to how lonely it must have been for him, I would let them know that being an only child forces kids to reach out to create friends. My son had more friends and sleep-overs than I care to count. He became a friendly, well adjusted, popular guy, who never felt slighted in any way for being the only child. When one has one, college expenses are feasible, a car at graduation is feasible, clothes, and extra clubs and sports teams are all affordable. I knew my limitations and I knew that, as a teacher, my finances would be limited, so one child was perfect for me.

Education

I also was pretty forceful when it came to the "Life Lessons" explaining to my girls that if you have no financial options, you may feel you have to stay with a man who will bully and abuse, not only you, but your innocent children as well. The plight of the women of the fifties was just that. As stay at home moms, if one was not happy, it was a rarity where a woman could leave. Where would she go and with what money? I would explain the importance of an education to ensure that escape from a bad situation would definitely be an option.

So many girls had babies at the tender ages of fourteen, fifteen, or sixteen. I noted that their emotional growth was pretty much arrested when they gave birth, because they considered themselves "grown". They also acquired a sort of "mama" status with their peers. Also, it was a rare girl who cared about losing the baby weight. The boys would move on and the girl's life would now be, not ruined, but forever complicated.

I recall a pregnant girl who attended her prom with her "baby daddy". She shared with me that her mother was so very proud of her for waiting until her senior year to become pregnant. She and the baby's father were special education students, who both were barely literate.

Chapter 14

Nothing lasts forever

Nothing lasts forever. All good things must come to an end. And it did. My last assignment was in the most infamous high school in the area. The building looked like a prison from the street. It was a relatively new building that was air conditioned and air tight. This was an area with heavy drug trafficking. The police, fire, and teachers were all regarded as being at risk. During my five years at this school I was stopped for speeding three times by the police, on my way to school. Each time, when I divulged my destination, I was let go with a heartfelt, "Good luck, and try to have a safe day". What people who don't work where we work don't know is that kids are kids. For the most part, if one is nice to them, they'll be nice back. I always had the mindset that they were not out to get me. They were out to get each other.

I had been welcomed with open arms and made some of the most long lasting relationships of my life. The head of the English department was an older woman who was a victim of polio as a child, and wore leg braces. She helped me a lot and also warned me that many of the new people to the building spend a lot of their first year out sick. They thought it was some sort of a curse. This held true for me as well. Every fall I would get what I liked to call my "fall sore throat" that would stay with me until June. My practical reasoning was that after being off all summer, upon returning to my stage, I over-used my voice. Also, I was a terminal hugger. I usually promised myself that I would quit the hugging because I was contracting all those kids' germs and carrying them with me all year long. This "fall sore throat" was also prevalent while I was employed at the detention center. I turned fifty while in the detention center and I attributed my dark circles and my lethargy to aging. As the years went by, I was noticing that my symptoms were becoming worse and I had more of them. It would start with my "fall sore throat" that wasn't bad enough to bother seeking medical help. I really thought it was the result of over use. I always had a Kleenex in my hand for the purpose of blowing my nose and wiping my draining eyes. Here is my ever expanding list of symptoms: heart palpitations, heated face but no temperature, itchy skin, coughing, shaking, shortness of breath, and ringing in my ears. I was powering through every day. When my throat and cough would become so bad that I had to seek medical help, the news was always the same, a sinus infection and bronchitis, requiring antibiotics for ten days. I was usually unable to go to school for two weeks at a time, because I would completely lose my voice. There were times when I couldn't even make the call to the substitute center, because I was unable to talk. My doctor was baffled. I was taking so many antibiotics that I was in clear danger of becoming immune to them. I would return to school and the chaos my absence had caused, and be fine for a few days . . . until the symptoms returned.

Finally, a light bulb went off for my doctor and he referred me to an allergist that was right down the hall from his office. I was so excited to maybe get to the bottom of this mystery illness. When I arrived, she had a chart for me to fill out listing all my symptoms, of which almost all were checked off. I told her where I worked and said that special attention should maybe be given to mold and mildew. Our underground parking lot was quite a breeding ground for mold and mildew, and I was hoping for those to be the culprits. She did the battery of hundreds, it seemed, of pricks to the skin all up and down my arms and all over my back. This test introduced into my skin every matter imaginable, and then I waited for about thirty minutes until inevitable reactions manifested. I was sitting in this room in total agony awaiting her and a possible answer to the cause of my misery. When she returned, she had an answer. She told me that there was only one thing the "exploded" on my back . . . . I have an allergy to cockroaches! No mold. No mildew. Cockroaches! It took me a minute to absorb this ugly information. I cried. She sympathized. She said we can fix this. I assured her that the school had regular extermination, but she then informed me that my allergy is to the droppings of the cockroaches and their dead bodies that turn to dust in the air that I'm breathing. Since this building was air tight due to the air conditioning, this funky air was being recycled each and every day. The air tight situation in the slammer was the exact same thing, in that the windows were never opened. I only had to make it to the end of the school year and then my summers were cockroach-free. She prescribed allergy meds that worked beautifully overnight.

The other half of my cure, according to this allergist, was to receive weekly injections for a couple of years with the goal of immunity to these nasty cockroaches. Now, I knew that retirement was right around the corner for me, so I was leery about having these injections. In my fifties I'd become extremely conscious of what I was putting into my body. When I asked to have an appointment with this doctor regarding the long term ramifications of these injections, she skirted the issue to say the least. I reminded her that by the time the immunity would be kicking in, I would be retiring. She was not happy with me. I reluctantly continued with these injections, until the time came when they upped the dosage and I saw that what was being injected into my body was green! Green cockroach juice! That was the end of it for me . . . and summer was coming.

I was healthy for the entire summer. Three days after returning to school I was sick. I called her office and asked for the prescription and she refused, claiming that I needed to have an appointment. The appointment was made for a week later and by then I was in full blown agony. On my way up the elevator to her office, I ran into a father with his two kids who were familiar to me because they were among those there on the appointed injection days with everyone else. These injections were administered by her nurse. The doctor was not even around. When I asked this father what his kids were receiving these shots for, he said, "Cockroach allergies"! Is it really that common?

I entered her office ill, with an attitude. She blamed me for not continuing those green injections. I told her that she seemed to be running some sort of a scam around these weekly injections. The stream of patients was never ending on those days, and the insurance companies were paying for each and every appointment. Just think how much money she was making with these people believing they needed these shots for years to become ultimately immune! I demanded my records and told her I was done. She escorted me to her main desk and loudly enough for all in the office to hear she asked me if there was anything else she could do for me. I still believe that there are not that many people in need of weekly injections. I questioned her and she didn't like it. She just wanted me to shut up and keep coming for years.

I called my retirement people only to find that I was, indeed, eligible to go out on a sick leave and then retire. A transfer was out of the question, because there was no guarantee of finding a cockroach-free school. I went with the plan. Every teacher accumulates sick days from year to year. I had accumulated well over one hundred days, that would have turned into cash upon retirement, however, in order to reach my legal retirement date, I had to use them up. It would have been over $10,000. I walked out of my classroom on Halloween and never returned. I've always felt that I had abandoned my students, however, there was absolutely no way I could carry on. I was sick of being sick.

I was advised to go through workman's compensation to see if I had a case to regain the moneys I'd lost. I would have easily worked another five years. After all, the cockroaches were not my fault. I attended two court hearings, neither to any avail. The end result was that I was found to have had a pre-existing condition. What? I was unwilling to continue fighting the machine. I gave up. I retired. I have grandchildren, a part time job as a receptionist in an all female law office, and I maintain my nail hobby/business out of my home. I'm fine, however, I still have melancholy moments where I miss the stage, the attention, the love, and the hugs. I miss my sweet wildflowers.

The End

About the Author

Born and raised in the Midwest, Judy enjoys spending time with her grandsons, family, and friends. She works as a part-time receptionist for five female attorneys while maintaining her relaxing hobby as a nail tech for her friends.

This book was the result of wanting to share her stories and her knowledge with those who may want to pursue a teaching career and for those who have been, or who have had, a teacher.

For years people have urged her to put her stories in print. On his deathbed, her father had her promise to write this book.

CPSIA information can be obtained at www.ICGtesting.com
Printed in the USA
BVOW05s0456091214

378539BV00004B/31/P